REFRESHING GRAMMAR

An easy-going guide for teachers,
writers and other creative people

Jodie Clark

GFD

Copyright © 2023 Jodie Clark

All rights reserved

No part of this book may be reproduced, or stored in a retrieval system, or transmitted in any form or by any means, electronic, mechanical, photocopying, recording, or otherwise, without express written permission of the publisher.

The author has asserted her right to be identified as the author of this work in accordance with the Copyright, Designs and Patents Act 1988.

ISBN 979-8-399-05669-2

To the participants on the Refreshing Grammar course. Your generous commitment to making learning a space of welcome, creativity and fun is what inspired me to write this book.

CONTENTS

Title Page
Copyright
Dedication
1 Introduction — 1
2 Clause and effect — 11
3 Stick to the subject — 24
4 While we're on the subject — 39
5 Verb vibes — 55
6 Non-finite resources — 75
7 Too tense to be in the mood — 88
8 With my complements (for the overachievers) — 100
9 Adding junk with adjuncts — 112
10 Grammar for dreamers — 121
Appendix 1 Word class for teachers with class — 129
Appendix 2 Passive voice (brought to you by zombies) — 139
Answers to the exercises — 143
Notes — 152
About The Author — 161

1 INTRODUCTION

Trusting your linguistic intuition

Do you know everything you need to know about grammar?

Spoiler alert: this is a trick question. The answer is "yes."

Even if you don't know where to stick your commas. Even if you don't know the difference between a gerund and a present participle. Even if you don't know how to pronounce the word *gerund*.

My intention with this book is to help you access your "linguistic intuition," a term used to describe your unconscious knowledge about the structure of language. There's a fair amount of discussion in the linguistics community about this unconscious knowledge, where it comes from, how to access it, what it should be called. My own interest in the term stems from over 20 years of experience of teaching English at university level, listening to my students' fears about their introductory linguistics classes.

They struggled with the grammar. They found it so hard that they were questioning whether they were smart enough to be on the degree.

I needed a way to build the confidence of these

students, and I wondered if thinking in terms of "linguistic intuition" might be the way in. So I got to work. I doubled down on my favourite approach to grammar, called Systemic Functional Grammar (or SFG), developed by M.A.K. Halliday,[1] which I like for lots of reasons, not least because it's intuitive. I took note of Thomas and Meriel Bloor's explanation of how various "probes" in SFG help us access what we know about grammatical structure.[2] And I experimented with different starting points in introducing the components of language, finally deciding (controversially) that the best place to begin is at the level of the clause. (More on that in Chapter 2).

With these tools in hand, I developed a new approach to studying grammar that empowered students, and I started delivering it with a light, irreverent touch.

It worked. The students got it. They got it so well that they started getting curious, asking interesting questions, making and delighting in new discoveries about language and using their new knowledge to fuel their creativity. In feedback forms, students remarked on how much this method of approaching grammar improved their confidence, and how much fun they had.

The results were too good to keep to myself, so I decided to share my methods with fellow educators. I extended the approach to UK secondary teachers in a course called Refreshing Grammar, after which this book is named. (The course is now available to everyone who's interested, not just teachers, and you can sign up for free at jodieclark.com/refreshingcourse.) Participants' responses to that course were even more inspiring than the feedback from my undergraduates. The keyword that kept coming up was *confident.*

"This course has greatly enhanced my confidence and ability to teach grammar at A-Level," one Refreshing Grammar participant said. Another revealed, "My colleague has also completed the course and we have spent lots of hours after school applying the tools to clauses so that we can develop our own confidence and knowledge."

Even teachers who were already grammar savvy appreciated the new approach. Isobel, head of her school's English department said, "Refreshing Grammar offered new strategies and ways of thinking which I genuinely went into the classroom the next day and applied. I was fairly confident about grammar but found Jodie's approach much more intuitive, as did our students."

Talk about inspiring! I'm very grateful to the many students and teachers who've been open to this new approach to grammar, and I'm thrilled to have this opportunity to share it even more widely.

Relaxed, messy, fun

Did you get to take art classes in school, and if so, did you enjoy them? I look back to my middle school art classroom as an oasis in a desert of adolescent despair. The smell of tempera and wet clay, the jubilant displays of papier mâché sculptures hanging on metal hooks suspended from plasterboard ceiling tiles, the high wooden tables splattered with a chaotic palette of spilt paint, the metal stools on which we perched unselfconsciously, focusing on our creative endeavours.

There was no rule in art class about not talking to our neighbours. Conversations weren't seen as disruptive or unruly, just a natural by-product of the creative process. As we sketched, painted, sculpted and pasted, we admired each other's work, offered suggestions and gossiped about our lives.

When I reflect upon the learning atmosphere I'd love to create for both my students and myself, it's the energy of the art classroom that comes to mind. Relaxed, messy, chatty, fun and oriented toward making new things. This is the learning atmosphere I'm trying to create with this book.

Relaxed, messy, fun... I recognise these are not adjectives you might expect to accompany a textbook on grammar. Even mentioning a technical word like *adjective* may have thrown you straight out of the creative vibes of the art room—either because you're "no good" at grammar (*Wait. What's an adjective, again?*), or else potentially because you're "too good" at grammar (*Isn't fun a noun? Can't relaxed be a verb?*). And even if you're someone who does find grammar fun, it might involve the same type of pleasure I get from pulling the dandelions from my flowerbeds. There's a certain smug satisfaction in feeling like you're in control of a chaotic environment.

If that's the kind of fun you have with grammar, you're probably also dubious about "messy."

That said, the impetus for this book and the approach I'll be sharing here derive from how my own career as a linguist has developed. My love affair with language began when I studied young people's use of the word *like* in everyday conversation.[3] (Talk about messy.) Recently I've been writing fiction[4] and recording podcasts[5] to explore what I think are the more mysterious aspects of language. (Talk about fun.) I've peppered this book with writing prompts to encourage you open your mind to the possibility that grammar doesn't have to be a red pen making angry marks across your writing, pointing out your manifold errors.

It could also be a set of *art supplies*.

Everything you need to know?

Will *Refreshing Grammar* tell you where to put your commas? Will it stop you from misplacing possessive apostrophes?

No. This book doesn't address the conventions of written language, such as punctuation and spelling, which generally follow *prescriptive* rules of grammar. We'll be using a *descriptive* approach in this book, which means we're treating the "rules" of grammar as patterns to be discovered, in the same way that biologists might seek to discover which gene combinations produce particular traits. A descriptive approach recognises that there are many varieties of every language, and that all varieties have their own structures.

A prescriptive approach, on the other hand, assumes there's only one right way to speak or write a given language. The "correct" way conforms to the structures of whichever variety was selected through a process of social and political struggle as the "standard" form of that language.

Prescriptive approaches to grammar are problematic for lots of reasons, but mostly because they contribute to what I think of as "grammar shaming." To be grammar shamed is to be told there's something fundamentally wrong with the way you've expressed yourself. The implication is often that there's something wrong with you: you're not smart enough, you're not well educated enough, you're not savvy enough, you're not "in the know," you don't have the right kind of cultural capital and/or you shouldn't be taking up space on whatever platform you're using.

But I'm a teacher, I hear you say. *I need my students to know the rules of punctuation. The curriculum demands it!*

I'm a writer, I hear you say. *I need to know the rules so that people don't think I'm a fraud.*

Teachers, writers, creative wordsmiths—this book is for you. I understand that you need to know "the rules." But I'd like to offer you something even better.

A participant on the Refreshing Grammar course put it beautifully. "What I love about Refreshing Grammar is its approach, which is a revelation to me, and which really suits the way I like to learn. It has opened up a world of language in a way that hasn't been available to me. And the grammar textbooks suddenly make better sense."

Opened up a world. I delighted to hear it. Analysing grammatical structures has opened up many new worlds to me, and in Chapter 10 I'll relate my own experiences of how the grammar of people's stories helped me understand how we could shape more welcoming worlds. But let's set aside those lofty thoughts for now and put our attention on the grammar textbooks that "suddenly made better sense."

What if you had so much confidence in your knowledge of the basic principles of grammar that you could google the answers to your specific language questions and quickly understand the answers you get? (As someone with a PhD in linguistics and decades of research behind me, I'm not ashamed to tell you that I still ask google questions about language on the daily.) My intention with this book is not to provide a definitive or exhaustive guide to English grammar, but instead to build your confidence, to empower you to probe more deeply when you need to, and most importantly, to have fun along the way.

How the book is structured

Refreshing Grammar is a clause-based approach, and each chapter is designed not only to help you identify the elements of a clause in English, but also to understand the multifaceted aspects of these elements. What's more, I'll be encouraging you to *play* with these structures, by analysing literary works and getting creative with writing prompts.

Chapter 2, "Clause and effect," gives some background to my decision to use clauses as a starting point for grammatical study. It also illustrates how linguistic intuition works in a three-year-old, even one caught in the grip of intense moral indignation.

Chapter 3, "Stick to the subject," introduces the crowning jewel of the Refreshing Grammar approach, which I call the "question-tag probe" (also known as a mood tag).[6] The question-tag probe has been a game changer for everyone I've taught who's ever been confused by grammatical structure... and even for people who aren't confused. As one participant on the course remarked, "The question-tag probe is a revelation. Such a simple yet effective starting point for myself and my students to use." Once you've learned how to use the probe to find the subject of a clause, you'll go on in Chapter 4 ("While we're on the subject") to explore subjects of clauses in more detail and analyse more complex or difficult cases.

In Chapter 5, "Verb vibes," you'll be delighted to learn that the question-tag probe can help you identify the verb element of a clause as well as the subject. Then, in Chapters 6 ("Non-finite resources") and 7 ("Too tense to be in the mood") you'll explore how this tool can elucidate some of the nuances of verbs, like finiteness, agreement, mood and tense.

Chapter 8, "With my complements," introduces a new tool, the *who/what* probe, which can be used to find another clause element, the complement. You'll learn about transitive and intransitive verbs, and the difference between complements and objects. You'll also learn how to do something called SVCA analysis, which is a way of identifying all the elements of any given clause.

In Chapter 9, "Adding junk with adjuncts," you'll discover how to locate the final type of clause element, the adjunct. We'll play with the flexibility of these elements and come to the conclusion that they're not junk, after all.

Chapter 10, "Grammar for dreamers," is where we explore the possibility that understanding grammatical structures can open portals to creative new ideas in writing, teaching and life. And we'll do some dreaming.

Most chapters contain exercises to check your understanding and writing prompts to spark your creativity. The answers to the exercises are at the end of the book.

And, because I know that the teachers among you will ask for them… I've included appendices on the two things I get the most questions about: word class and passive voice.

But do you need a book about grammar?

Frankly? I don't believe you do. If you're here to improve your grammar, you're out of luck, because I think your grammar is perfect as it is. If you're here to impress (or annoy) your friends with your ability to spot a dangling participle, you're definitely reading the wrong book!

But maybe you're like me, as enchanted and enraptured by the mysteries of language as you are frustrated by what people say you're supposed to know about it. If you're in the teaching profession, you'll know exactly what I mean—you're probably grappling with frustrating curricular demands about the grammatical terminology your students are expected to command. You may, like me, wish to create an art room resonance in your classroom, but the requirement that you teach fronted adverbials kills that vibe straight away.

You may be someone who writes creatively. Whether it's poetry, fiction, non-fiction, screenplays, lyrics, blogs, scripts for videos, newsletters, copy to promote your business, journal entries, or anything else that comes to mind, you're using language as an expressive medium for your creative endeavours. Chances are you've experienced grammar shaming at some point along your path. I once heard a creative writing professor state with arrogant assuredness that "If you don't know how to use a semi-colon, people will just think you're stupid."

What? So much for messy. So much for easy-going. So much for fun. So much for the relaxed atmosphere of the art room. I think this guy went on to deliver a series of e-courses entitled "How to stultify your creativity in three easy steps."

This book is designed to inspire a sense of fun, curiosity and, most importantly, confidence when it comes to using language creatively and/or teaching others to do the same.

You don't have to be as language obsessed as I am to get value from this book. You really just need to be mildly curious, and a little bit fascinated. Whatever brought you here, thanks for coming. I can't wait to hear what this approach to grammar inspires you to create.

2 CLAUSE AND EFFECT

Words, words, words

Remember the scene in *Hamlet* where Polonius is trying to figure out if his daughter's boyfriend (Hamlet) is crazy, depressed or both? There's no indication in the play that Polonius has any psychiatric training, but he poses a series of diagnostic questions anyway. One of them is "What do you read, my lord?" (Hamlet's carrying a book.)

"Words," his daughter's suitor wearily replies. "Words, words, words."

Most people (including me) would probably agree with Polonius that "words" is not the normal, expected or appropriate response to someone asking what you're reading.

If that's the case, then why, I often wonder, do so many people think the study of grammar should begin with the study of words?

Or more specifically, word classes, also known as parts of speech. Do you need to be able to delineate the difference between an adjective and an adverb, make a list of concrete and abstract nouns, and spot all the verbs in a paragraph? These tests feel dreary and wearisome to me, for lots of reasons. One of them is that words consistently and obstinately defy naïve attempts to stick labels on them. Most words can very happily wear different word-class badges in different contexts, sometimes in the same sentence. My favourite example is *round*, which can be labelled as an adjective, an adverb, a noun, a verb and a preposition depending on how it shows up:

> A *round* (adjective) *table would look better in this room*
> *Samira and Jez came round* (adverb) *the other day*
> *I'll buy the next round* (noun) *of drinks*
> *Why don't we round* (verb) *9.67 up to 10?*
> *She'll be coming round* (preposition) *the mountain*

I have to disclose a particular affinity for the word *round*. I like anything that's brave enough to resist easy classification (*like* is another example). It's not actually the words that I take issue with. It's the unproblematised assumption that learning about grammar should start with labelling words.

As Kim Ballard points out in her book *The Frameworks of English* (which I'd recommend as a supplement to this book if you want something that's a bit more comprehensive and technical), most people think of words as the "building blocks" of language.[7] This may be because language is often associated with its written form, and spotting words on a page or screen is as easy as looking at the spaces between them. To get a clearer grasp of this, choose a language you have no knowledge of at all, like Dutch or Japanese, and search the internet for a text in that language. (Google "Japanese text," for instance.) Then have a look at one of the images that pops up. Chances are, even in languages that don't use the Latin alphabet, you'll be able to pick out individual words with reasonable success.

Now try Googling "someone speaking Japanese" (or whatever language you've chosen) and listen to the sound or video file that pops up. Can you identify any individual words?

I certainly can't. Even in French, which is a language I once had a pretty solid fluency in, I'd still make mistakes in identifying where one unfamiliar word ended and another began. My notes on a master's seminar on Chomsky, given in French at the University of Strasbourg, were full of references to *"illosyntaxiques."* I didn't know what these were, but the word sounded technical enough to be right. Turns out the term was *"îlots syntaxiques,"* syntactic islands, and the penny didn't drop until I read Chomsky in the original English. I feel bad for the guy who asked to borrow my notes...

A teaching dilemma

If you were lucky enough to study linguistics on some level, perhaps at university, perhaps through your own autodidactic exploration, you might have learned about the various components of language structure. These are phonemes (the individual sounds of a language), morphemes (units of meaning), words (single or combined morphemes), phrases (groups of words), clauses (groups of phrases), sentences (single or combined clauses) and texts (meaningful groups of sentences). If you've been formally trained in linguistics, you may have started with phonemes and worked your way up. At school, as we've already discussed, you probably started with words, maybe making reference to morphemes (roots, prefixes and suffixes) along the way. You may have learned, for instance, that the bound morpheme -*ness*, when added to the end of an adjective (like *good*), produces a noun (*goodness*).

When I first started teaching introductory linguistics to first-year English students, I learned straight away not to start at the smallest component of language—phonemes. To learn phonology (the study of phonemes), you have to first become familiar with the International Phonetic Alphabet, which can feel like learning a whole new language. Then you get shown a cross-section of the vocal apparatus (the mouth, nasal cavity and larynx), and get tasked with figuring out how these body parts interact to produce the different sounds of whatever language you're studying.

Some folks are really excited to learn that the sound at the beginning of the word *fig* is a voiceless labiodental fricative, but most of my students couldn't give, well, a fig.

So I experimented with starting my introductory linguistics courses at other levels of the structural hierarchy. My attempt at making morphology fun involved multicoloured notecards with free and bound morphemes on them. My students pretended to find this interesting, but I wasn't fooled.

Starting with words classes was also a wash, for the reasons I've given already. Also, it didn't seem intuitive to anyone that *depression* was the noun form of the word *depress* (verb). When students tried to get their heads around that, they just got *depressed* (adjective).

Another year, another attempt—this time I decided to start with phrases. I extracted paragraphs from whimsical blogs written by other university first-years and asked the students to spot the noun phrases in them.

I thought this would be more intuitive than word class, because you can test whether something is a noun phrase (like, *a problem with my big toe*) by replacing it with a pronoun (like, *it*). But phrases are like Russian dolls—they often hide other phrases within them. So in the sentence *I have a problem with my big toe*, you could say *I have a problem with it*, which tells you that *my big toe* is a noun phrase. But you could also say *I have it*, which tells you that *a problem with my big toe* is also a noun phrase. Oh, and so is *I*.

I is a noun phrase. Even though it doesn't have any nouns in it. Don't @ me.

I've discovered an unspoken (most of the time) division in the various English departments I've been associated with in various parts of the world. The assumption is that among the people who study English, some are naturally good at linguistics, and some will never get it. People in the former group are detail oriented, scientifically minded and disarmingly organised. People in the latter group are imaginative, creative, insightful and can produce at least one cold mug of half-full, mould-covered coffee from behind their overflowing bookshelves.

If you majored in English (or are majoring in it now), you may have already situated yourself in one of the above categories. You may have scraped your way through the compulsory "language" section of your degree, doing the bare minimum so you could focus on Romantic poetry or creative writing. Or, if you're in the other camp, you might have found solace in the structured approach most linguistics classes take. It might have been, well, *nice* to know that even in descriptive approaches to grammar you'd find a phenomenon absent from the more literary and creative classes—definitive answers.

If I bought into the "two camps" theory of English majors, I'd have given up after my failed attempt to make phrases fun. The folks who were always going to love grammar were going to find language study fun regardless of how many coloured notecards I used. And the folks who were going to hate it were destined to hate it, and no attempt at lightening the load would help.

But what about art class? I kept thinking. No one in my middle school art class worried about whether we were any good at art. We just relished the opportunity to get our hands dirty and make things.

Yes, but none of us grew up to be the next Van Gogh, either. And besides, grammar isn't art class.

And then I had a conversation with a three-year-old that changed everything.

What a three-year-old taught me about grammar

Actually, she was two years and eight months old, and she didn't fall into either of the camps I just described. She wasn't even destined to be an English major—she recently graduated with a degree in chemical engineering. She's my niece, Elli,[8] and I once recorded a conversation we had back in 2003.

I was supposed to by looking after Elli and her baby brother Jake, but as you'll see, I was doing a better job in the self-appointed role as field linguist than as caregiver for young children. The three of us were sitting on the floor surrounding by building blocks.

(What a great setting to discover something about the building blocks of language.)

I'm not sure what I'd focused my attention on at the time, but clearly there was some sort of sibling altercation that had slipped completely under my radar. Something about block theft. I present the following transcript as evidence:

> Elli: *Jake take my blocks away!*
> Jodie: *Did he? Here. ((turning aside)) Why don't you take some of these*
> Elli: *((taking the blocks out of Jake's hand?)) No, Jake! No!*
> Jodie: *((turning back)) Oh, thanks for giving it back Jake. Thank you!*
> Elli: *Elli give it back by myself.*

When I show this transcript to students, usually in the context of sessions on language acquisition, they are quick to point out what's wrong with Elli's utterances —that her subjects don't agree with her verbs, that the verbs are in the wrong tense, that she sometimes refers to herself in the third person and that she confuses *give* with *take*.

Isn't it interesting that the first impulse when analysing someone's language is so often to spot what's wrong? It's another illustration of the pervasiveness of grammar shaming.

But child language acquisition experts can't afford to fall into the grammar-shaming trap. Instead they must adopt the objective stance that is necessary for any linguistic research. That means finding ways to identify the linguistic structures that children *have* acquired in addition to those they haven't. And while Elli at two years and eight months might not be an expert on verb tense, she's got one thing nailed pretty well.

She knows her way around a clause.

Quantum language leaps

What's a clause? We touched on it earlier when we discussed the structural hierarchy of language components. A clause is a group of phrases.
   Is it really as simple as that?
   No, it's not. (Sorry.)
   If we take the last thing that Elli says in the above transcript and divide it into phrases, it looks something like this:

Elli (noun phrase)
give (verb phrase)
it (noun phrase)
back (adverb phrase)
by myself (prepositional phrase)
myself (noun phrase)

Now if this list causes some confusion for you, I get it. Aren't phrases supposed to be groups of words? So why do most of those phrases consist of only one word? Why is *back* an adverb phrase?[9] Why is *myself* a noun phrase?
   How on earth am I supposed to learn all this nonsense?
   To which I would say, maybe you don't need to learn all this nonsense to have a good working knowledge of the structure of language. Elli certainly didn't know it, but that didn't stop her from forming utterances that were remarkably effective in signalling to me the travesty of justice that was occurring in her world at the time. (Not entirely effective, of course, given that she had to rely on extralinguistic strategies to give the blocks back by herself.)
   For now it's enough to notice that a collection of

phrases does not automatically constitute a clause. For instance, *back by myself* is a group of phrases, but it isn't a clause.

Linguist M. A. K. Halliday, whose systemic functional approach to grammar is the one I use in this book, describes a clause a "a quantum of information."[10] In physics, *quantum* means something like "the smallest thing." We've already said that the smallest component of language is the phoneme, or speech sound. But Halliday is referring here to how *information* is packaged, not just how language is structured. For Elli, the smallest unit of information requires her to tell me at least two things: (a) who or what's involved in the scene she's describing and (b) what they're doing (or being, or feeling, etc.), or what's being done to them.

Clauses can consist of as many as four elements, specifically subject (S), verb (V), complement (C) and adjunct (A), but at the minimum they must at least have a subject and a verb.

Don't worry too much about this terminology for now. In the next chapter I'm going to share my favourite technique for identifying subjects and verbs, and later in the book you'll discover why I'm using the term "complement" rather than "object." (It's not to confuse you, I promise.) Before long even the most complex or mystifying aspects of clause structure are going to feel like, well, child's play. At the moment I'll just ask you to notice what Elli knows (without knowing that she knows it) about clause structure.

Take her first utterance: *Jake take my blocks away!* It's a clause, a quantum of information in which Elli is situating a message about the injustice of her current experience. Despite its apparent simplicity, the clause contains all the clause elements, not just the requisite subject and verb:

Subject (S): Jake
Verb (V): take
Complement (C): my blocks
Adjunct (A): away

What's more, Elli produces these in exactly the order you'd expect for a clause in English: SVCA. (This is not the only well formed order of clause elements, but it's the "unmarked" order, or the "default.")

The other clause we've looked at does exactly the same thing, only this time she's included a second adjunct:

S: Elli
V: give
C: it
A: back
A: by myself

What's worth noticing here is that even though not everything she says is what most would consider "correct" English, the clause structure is perfectly in place. To illustrate this point, let's work with a slightly more elaborate version of *Jake take my blocks away*. Imagine a scenario of unprecedented toddler eloquence, where Elli asserts something like "My self-entitled thug of a brother has stolen my treasured possessions for the last time."

Once we've caught that moment on video and posted it on social media, we might then take a step back to recognise that its clause structure is an exact parallel to *Jake take my blocks away*.

S: My self-entitled thug of a brother

V: has stolen
C: my treasured possessions
A: for the last time

There's nothing stopping us from imagining even more elaborate expressions that still adhere to this structure:

S: The snivelling excuse for a sibling that my parents produced without my approval
V: will have embezzled
C: those few humble tokens that I dare call my own
A: without the smallest hint of remorse

I have to admit, coming up with that last clause was kind of fun. The sense of endless possibility offered me a bit of the "art room" quality that I'm always striving for.

Writing prompt: give it back by yourself

Have a go at designing your own absurdly complicated version of the *Jake take my blocks away* structure and see if you have fun, too.

Now take a closer look at that last sentence:

The snivelling excuse for a sibling that my parents produced without my approval will have embezzled those few humble tokens that I dare call my own without the smallest hint of remorse.

Imagine trying to isolate any of the other levels of structure we've discussed so far. The thought of doing a "phrase spotting" exercise here boggles even my linguistically trained mind, let alone trying to label the classes of all 32 of the words.

But as you'll discover as you make your way through this book, clause analysis is done through a sort of higher-level chunking process, where you only have to identify at most four chunks (subject, verb, complement or adjunct). The chunks can be ginormous, and they can contain all manner of things in them, including other clauses, as you might have noticed. But as I've discovered with hundreds of students, clause chunking is a lot easier and more fun than word or phrase spotting… and I believe it ends up being more useful, depending on what you're trying to do. For most of the stuff I do with language, even just identifying subjects and verbs is enough. But if you decide you do want to look at a more granular level (Halliday uses the wonderful word "delicate" to describe more finely tuned analysis),[11] I believe it's easier to do the big-scale chunking first, and then have a closer look within each chunk.

Teaching dilemma, solved!

What I learned about grammar from my almost three-year-old niece was that the most relaxed, easy-going, fun and enjoyable place to start learning about the structure of language was at the level of the clause. Maybe I've convinced you to start there too. But I'm imagining you have all sorts of other questions, like *Why have I never come across these exact terms before?* and *Surely students need at least a working knowledge of nouns, verbs, etc. to get started?* and *What's an adjunct?* and *What are the criteria by which you identify all these elements* and most importantly…

I thought you said this was going to be fun?

We'll address all these questions as we go, but the last question (which is more of a comment, really) is the most important. So we'll prioritise it in the next chapter.

Exercise: Happy bracketing

The following clauses all have the same structure as (S Jake) (V take) (C my blocks) (A away). Have a go at putting brackets around the different clause elements. Don't worry about labelling them with SVCA just yet. You'll learn how to do that in Chapter 8.

A warning before you go on your happy bracketing way. Out of all the exercises in the book, this first one is possibly the hardest. (Not the best of pedagogic strategies, I realise.) Bear with me. Your brain knows how to bracket the clause elements, but you haven't yet learned how to access what your brain knows. You'll learn that as you go.

1. My three-year-old niece can express her views without difficulty
2. People on social media have been shaming me about my use of apostrophes
3. Most of my students couldn't give a fig about voiceless labiodental fricatives
4. This clause labelling exercise is stressing me now
5. I will be imbibing my favourite beverage as a result

3 STICK TO THE SUBJECT

As angry as an angry thing

Do you have a ritual that separates your creative writing from the more mundane tasks your busy life presents? Is putting your phone on silent enough to coax the words from your pen or keyboard? Is it the buzz of your favourite café and the earthy smell of roast coffee beans? Perhaps you light a scented candle, take a cleansing breath and post a sign on the door to your home office that reads DO NOT COME IN EXCEPT IN AN EMERGENCY. DO NOT COME IN TO ASK IF IT'S AN EMERGENCY.

For me the process involves sitting at my desk, setting a timer for a half hour, and pulling out a set of coloured pencils to make me feel like I'm in an art room. (My chair, by the way, is a raised metal stool and my desk is a 1950s draughting table my husband and I found in an antique shop many years ago. Let this picture remove any lingering doubts about my commitment to the art room vibe.)

Once I've decorated my large, messy, unlined white journal with the expansive circling strokes of a few coloured pencils, I feel ready to get to work.

Get to work... on what exactly?

How do you get started? Do you set yourself a writing goal? Do you write to a daily (or hourly) word count? Do you stare into the middle distance and wait for inspiration?

What works best for me is having a writing prompt, usually one I've designed myself, that will allow me to achieve whatever's required for the project. For my Grammar for Dreamers newsletter the prompt is something like "find a way to link my thoughts about Valentine's Day to the topic of last month's podcast episode."[12] For fiction it might be something like, "The character's alone in a room. Find a way to let the reader know she's angry and confused."

Then comes the part that, frankly, isn't really that much fun.

Trying to write it.

All the false starts. How do you write about someone who's angry?

She was angry.

It's not exactly Shakespeare, but I'm not trying to be Shakespeare, right? I'm just writing to the prompt. Let me try a metaphor.

She was as angry as... an angry thing.

Which angry thing? What things are angry?

She was as angry as an angry bear.

Oops. Used *angry* twice.

She was as angry as a bear who's being stung by a swarm of bees.

Wait. It's the bees who are angry in that scenario, right?

She was as angry as a swarm of bees disturbed by a hungry bear.

When did my story become *Winnie the Pooh*? Except not as well written as *Winnie the Pooh*.

Let me try showing, not telling. How do I "show" that someone's angry?

Her lip quivered ~~in anger~~. Her hands formed fists ~~of rage~~. Her face turned a raging red.

Can she see her own face? Is she looking in a mirror? Should I get up off my stool and look in the mirror, to see what my face looks like when it's angry? Are those wrinkles on my face? Should I buy something to fix that? Let me just check The Body Shop website for deals.

Thirty minutes later and thirty quid lighter: Glad that's sorted. Now. What was I trying to do again? Write about an angry character. And there was something about a hungry bear. Speaking of hunger, what about lunch? Maybe something with honey?

Would you believe me if I told you that grammar is a great way to break free of this type of time-sinking, creativity-sucking procrastination?

The grammatical players

Stick with me for just a moment. Have a look at the way Eudora Welty, in a short story called "A Piece of News," describes a character who's alone in a room, feeling angry and confused.

She said nothing more and, backing against the door, pushed it closed with her hip. Her anger passed like a remote flare of elation. Neatly avoiding the table where the coffee bag stood, she began to walk around the room, as if a teasing indecision, an untouched mystery, led her by the hand.[13]

I've shared this passage with hundreds of students and as many teachers hoping to inspire their own students, and most people think it's good writing. I think it's very good writing. It's certainly better than *She was as angry as a bear. Her lip quivered. Her hands formed fists*, etc.

Knowing that Eudora Welty writes better than me isn't exactly motivating. I need to know *exactly* what it is that makes the Welty passage better than my own, so that I can learn from her technique. And while there are many lenses with which to view the strategies she's using, the one that I've found most helpful (and fun) is the lens of grammar.

I start by dividing the passage into clauses. Specifically, I'm looking at the finite clauses, which you'll learn more about later.

There are five finite clauses in the passage, numbered below.

1. She said nothing more
2. and, backing against the door, pushed it closed with her hip
3. Her anger passed like a remote flare of elation
4. Neatly avoiding the table where the coffee bag stood, she began to walk around the room
5. as if a teasing indecision, an untouched mystery, led her by the hand

The next step for me is to identify the subject element and verb element of each clause. Remember: a clause can have any combination of four different elements, but the subject and verb are the only essential ones, which is why I focus so much on these. You'll also remember from the chunking exercises we did with Elli's conversation that clause elements can be as small as one word and as large as many words (to be precise).

You're going to get very, very good at finding the subject (S) and verb (V) elements of clauses (if you're not already), but for now I'll just give you the answers:
1. (S She) (V said)
2. (S She) (V pushed)
3. (S Her anger) (V passed)
4. (S she) (V began [to walk])
5. (S a teasing indecision, an untouched mystery) (V led)

Does anything catch your attention about this bit of writing when your focus is limited to subjects and verbs? Remember that the clause is the smallest unit of information that tells us two things: (a) who or what is involved in the scene and (b) what they're doing (or being, or feeling, etc.). Just looking at the subjects and verbs gives us a pretty clear picture of who the players are in Welty's scene (the subjects) and what they're doing (the verbs).[14]

But surely we already knew who the players were? You knew it before you even read the extract, because I told you that Welty had written about a character who was alone in a room. Which means she's the only one in the scene, right?

And sure enough, three of the five subjects in the above analysis are indeed the word *she*. When we add the verbs to these subjects we see this person moving around the room she's in—*pushing* and *walking*.

But the grammatical analysis points to more players

than just *she*. There are two other subjects: *Her anger* and *a teasing indecision, an untouched mystery*. It's as though the structure of these clauses is inviting us to see the emotions and states of being (*anger, indecision* and *mystery*) as moving around the room with her—*passing* and *leading*.

It turns out the fictional room is not mostly empty, with just one person in it. Instead it's teeming with emotions. The woman is moving among them and eventually being pulled away by them.

Focusing on the subjects and verbs of the clauses in passages of writing I admire has been a game changer for me. It encourages me to think about my own writing in a new way. Imagining that there's something I want to express—like a character's anger and confusion—makes me feel like I'm trying to paint something with only one colour. When I shift to thinking in terms of the literally infinite possibilities of subjects, verbs and their combinations, then a boundless palette of pigments spreads itself before me, and I get to choose the ones that most delight me.

Messy. Easy-going. Fun.

Probing questions

So now I'm imagining that you're so overwhelmed by the creative possibilities of grammatical analysis that you've pulled all your favourite books from your shelves, burrowed down to your favourite passages, and are now ripping apart the clauses with the unbridled delight of a puppy tackling an heirloom sofa.

And now I'm picturing your glee turning to despair as you realise exactly how complicated most pieces of writing actually are. Now you're writing a frustrated message to me, filled with questions. *What if a sentence has more than one clause? How do I know it has more than one clause? You said look for the finite clauses—what on earth are those? You said find the subject and verb—what if my clause has lots of verbs? Is the subject just one word, or can it be lots of words? Is the subject of the clause always the thing that comes first? Is the subject of the clause what the clause is about? What's the subject?*

If you really are asking those questions, I love you for it, and I'll answer most of them at various points along the way. The answers I don't give in this book you can find on the Refreshing Grammar resources page, which includes FAQs (jodieclark.com/refreshingresources). But please don't go there yet. (Or if you've gone there already, bookmark the page for later and come back here for now.)

Let's start with a question that we can deal with. *How do you find the subject of a clause?*

Many of my students would prefer me to start with *How do you* define *the subject of a clause?* But starting with definitions can be a tricky business. Kim Ballard defines the subject as "The element of a clause which precedes the verb and which is typically the agent of an active clause."[15] But subjects don't always come before verbs, and lots of other things can come before verbs that aren't the subject. Also, you'd need to understand what agents and active clauses are to make sense of this definition.[16]

M. A. K. Halliday, whose work on grammatical structures is mind-bogglingly comprehensive, writes that the subject "has always been one of the most obscure and controversial categories in western grammatical theory."[17] And if journeying into the labyrinth of grammatical controversy sounds enjoyable to you (I'll admit it sometimes does to me), then by all means have a look at Halliday's discussion of the subject in his book *On Grammar*. But we really don't have to go into the intricacies of grammatical subjects to locate them in a clause.

Think of it this way: you don't need to know the wavelengths of the colour green and its location on the visible spectrum to be able to point to green things in your environment. Your brain just knows what green is, and it has since you were a child.

Same thing, you'll be happy to hear, about the subjects of clauses. Your brain knows how to spot them.

The difference between colours and grammatical features is that we *know* we know how to spot colours and we *don't think we know* how to spot things like subjects and verbs. We've been conditioned by antiquated ideas in an oppressive education system that only the most intelligent people can fully grasp grammar.

But if that's the case, then how was it possible for my niece, at the age of two years and eight months, to have a complete command of the clause structure of English? I mean, I'm not saying my niece isn't intelligent; she's a chemical engineer, for goodness' sake. But she wasn't always smart enough to know her way around a carbon compound. When she was pushing three, her skill set was more or less limited to being adorable and knowing what was rightfully hers.

The more ways researchers find to safely explore the linguistic understanding of children and babies,[18] the more we're learning about how tuned in human beings are to grammatical structure, even before any of us have voiced our first word. It's deep in our brains, even if we don't have the right terminology (known as *metalanguage*) to describe it.

The good news is that there are ways of getting at the knowledge we've been in possession of since we were dribbling little cutie pies without even really having to learn anything new.

We can use clever little devices called *probes*.

If you're into science fiction, the idea of using a probe to access something in your brain may invoke unpleasant images of malevolent aliens. Sorry about that. When I teach about probes, I tend to use the image of one of those fairground games where a joystick-operated claw retrieves a cuddly toy trapped inside a plexiglass box. But grammatical probes are actually easier to use than toy claws and (I presume) extra-terrestrial examination devices.

Grammatical probes are simple ways to tap into your linguistic intuition, or what it is you know about the structure of your language, without necessarily knowing you know it.

I discovered my favourite probe when reading what linguists Thomas and Meriel Bloor wrote[19] about something that M. A. K. Halliday calls a "mood tag."[20]

I call it a "question-tag probe," and I love it so much I want to marry it.

Finding the subject should be easy, shouldn't it?

You're with me so far, aren't you? This is the best book on grammar you've ever read, isn't it? The ideas in it are actually really easy to grasp, aren't they?

You're starting to notice what I'm doing, aren't you?

I'm not starting to annoy you, am I?

OK, I'll stop now, I promise. As you'll have noticed, I turned the first five sentences in this section into questions by tagging two little words at the end. These structures are appropriately named *tag questions* or *question tags*, and they're often used in conversation to make sure the person you're talking to is tracking. Lots of research has been done on the function of question tags in conversation, but my favourite way to work with them is to use them as probes for finding the subject and verb elements of a clause.

Here's why I like them so much: they're simple. They're consistent. They're easy to use. And they work. Really, really well.

Try it out for yourself. Add a question tag to the end of each of the following clauses.

1. I have eaten all those chocolates
2. You were planning on giving them to Samira
3. Samira doesn't really like foodie gifts
4. Her brother agrees with me
5. Chocolate isn't her thing
6. You and I should buy something else for her
7. Bath smellies would be perfect

It was easy, wasn't it? (Sorry.) Here are the answers, in case you need them (but I bet you don't).

1. I have eaten all those chocolates, *haven't I?*
2. You were planning on giving them to Samira, *weren't you?*
3. Samira doesn't really like foodie gifts, *does she?*
4. Her brother agrees with me, *doesn't he?*
5. Chocolate isn't her thing, *is it?*
6. You and I should buy something else for her, *shouldn't we?*

7. Bath smellies would be perfect, *wouldn't they?*

Now have a look at all the question tags you were able to produce without even thinking about it, and see if you can identify any patterns in how they're structured.

1. haven't I
2. weren't you
3. does she
4. doesn't he
5. is it
6. shouldn't we
7. wouldn't they

As you've probably noticed, all the tags are comprised of two words. The first will always be a type of verb called an *auxiliary*, such as (from the above examples) *have, were, does, is, should* and *would*. In most tags, the auxiliary is accompanied by the reduced form of the word not (*n't*) —also known as a *negative particle*. The second and final word in the tag is always a pronoun—more specifically, a *subject pronoun*.

Want to know something amazing about subject pronouns? There are only seven of them in contemporary Standard English.[21]

Why does that matter? Because the number of ways to construct the subject element in a clause is literally infinite. And yet, despite this vertiginous immensity of possibilities, every subject element (with only a few minor exceptions) can be replaced with one of these seven subject pronouns.

So if you're unsure about which part of the clause is the subject element, all you have to do is check which string of words can be replaced with a subject pronoun.

But how do you know which subject pronoun you're supposed to replace it with?

You might not think you know. But your brain knows. Ask it to stick a question tag at the end of the clause. Or better yet, look at the ones your brain already produced for you in the chocolates clauses above. Your brain produced all the seven subject pronouns without any of the rest of you breaking into a sweat: *I, you, she, he, it, we* and *they*.

All you have to do now is take whichever subject pronoun your brain found in the question tag and check which part of the clause it's referring to, and what it can replace.

To test it out, we'll try an easy one from our examples above: *Bath smellies would be perfect.* The question tag, *wouldn't they* gives *they* as the subject pronoun that can replace the subject element of the clause. So all we have to do is check to see what *they* could replace.

In this clause, *they* replaces *bath smellies*.

So *bath smellies* is the subject.

Now, you'll have noticed that some of the subject pronouns in the question tags from examples above, like *I* and *you*, replace the same word in the clause. In those cases, the single pronoun is the subject. In the case of *You and I should buy something else for her*, the subject is *you and I* (which can be replaced by the pronoun in the question tag, *we*).

To bring it all together, have a look once more at the sentences and their question tags below. The subjects are **underlined and in bold**. The pronouns in the question tags are in **bold**.

1. **I** have eaten all those chocolates, *haven't **I**?*
2. **You** were planning on giving them to Samira, *weren't **you**?*
3. **Samira** doesn't really like foodie gifts, *does **she**?*

35

4. **Her brother** agrees with me, *doesn't **he**?*
  5. **Chocolate** isn't her thing, *is **it**?*
  6. **You and I** should buy something else for her, *shouldn't **we**?*
  7. **Bath smellies** would be perfect, *wouldn't **they**?*

Discovering this use of the question-tag probe has been the biggest game changer for me in teaching introductory linguistics. Suddenly identifying grammatical features became something everyone in the class could do with ease. I've shared this technique with hundreds of secondary teachers, who report using it in their classroom with great success. Their experience (and mine) is that it creates a bit of a buzz. A student struggling to find the subject can be reminded by their peers to use a question-tag probe, and they're instantly back on track. It's easy, empowering, and (dare I say it) fun.

But it can't really be as easy as that. (Can it?)

It's *mostly* as easy as that. But I will admit that I handpick my examples to make them as simple as possible, at least in the beginning. It's not always as easy when you're spotting subjects "in the wild."

But it's still pretty easy.

Have a look again at the clauses from the Eudora Welty story and see if you (and/or your students) can attach question tags to them and then find the subjects.

  1. She said nothing more
  2. and, backing against the door, pushed it closed with her hip
  3. Her anger passed like a remote flare of elation
  4. Neatly avoiding the table where the coffee bag

stood, she began to walk around the room
5. as if a teasing indecision, an untouched mystery, led her by the hand

Is this what you got?
1. **She** said nothing more, *did she?*
2. and, backing against the door, pushed it closed with her hip, *didn't she?*
3. **Her anger** passed like a remote flare of elation, *didn't it?*
4. Neatly avoiding the table where the coffee bag stood, **she** began to walk around the room, *didn't she?*
5. as if **a teasing indecision, an untouched mystery**, led her by the hand, *didn't it?*

In doing this exercise you may have noticed a couple of anomalies. For instance, clause 2 shares the same subject with clause 1. The two clauses together form a compound sentence. When the subject of the second clause in a compound sentence is the same as the first, it can be omitted.

You may also have noticed that the subject in Clause 5 seemed to have two bits to it—the teasing indecision bit and the untouched mystery bit. This is a feature known as apposition and you find it in constructions like "My sibling, the rock star." The second phrase is another way of saying the first phrase.

How were you supposed to know that?

Well, you weren't. The point of this book, as we've discussed, is not to make you an expert on every nuance of grammatical structure. It's to make you feel confident enough to have a good play with those structures.

Are you feeling confident yet?

If not, it may help to have a few more strategies

for navigating clauses with slightly less straightforward subjects. Never fear—that's exactly what we'll be doing in Chapter 4.

Exercise: Find the subject

Use the question-tag probe to help you find the subject element of the following clauses.
1. Eudora Welty was a Pulitzer Prize-winning author
2. My sweets-loving friends really want to get chocolates for Samira
3. Writing about anger can be a tricky business
4. The question-tag probe is changing my approach to grammar
5. M. A. K. Halliday calls the question-tag probe a "mood tag"
6. I have mentioned his work several times in this chapter

4 WHILE WE'RE ON THE SUBJECT

Curiouser and curiouser

I'm hoping that the previous chapter has convinced you that your brain is *very* good at finding the subjects of clauses. That said, you may have run into a few snags when doing the exercises. And if you've tried finding the subjects of all those complicated clauses that crop up in the wild, you might have decided it doesn't work as well as with the carefully cultivated examples that appear in grammar books.

It's true that the question-tag probe isn't 100% accurate (no probe is), but in my experience what most often keeps people from correctly identifying the subject of a clause isn't a question-tag probe failure. It's almost always because folks are resisting trusting their linguistic intuition. In other words, some misguided idea about what the subject is supposed to be has overridden what the question-tag probe has told them (if they've remembered to use the question-tag probe at all).

I believe these misguided assumptions stem from the larger, more pernicious assumption I've been encouraging you to challenge throughout this book:

that most people aren't very good at grammar. Even wordsmith Lewis Carroll falls into this trap, as we discover early on in *Alice's Adventures in Wonderland*, where the narrator accuses Alice of being so surprised that "for the moment she forgot to speak good English."[22]

Despite Carroll's impulse to grammar shame his own heroine, his distinctive writing style can be tapped to help us unpick some misguided assumptions about the subjects of clauses that we may have picked up as we've travelled down the rabbit hole (sorry) of our own educational journey. Let's have a look at each misguided assumption in turn.

Misguided assumption 1: The subject is who or what the clause is about

Even if you haven't read *Alice's Adventures in Wonderland* —even if you've never heard of it—I bet you can make a pretty good guess about what the book is about.

Erm, Alice? And her adventures in a place called Wonderland?

Ding ding ding! Give that contestant a reality-expanding, currant-topped cake.

And what if you were asked to guess what the first paragraphs of the first chapter were about? If your instinct is to say they're about Alice, you're two for two. In the opening to the book we're told where Alice is (on a grassy bank), what she's doing (nothing), how she's feeling (bored) and who's with her (her sister).

Alice, Alice, Alice.

The subject of the book is also the subject of the first couple of paragraphs of the book, and, as it happens, the subject of quite a lot of the clauses. But linguistic terminology can be tricky. The word *subject* as a technical, metalinguistic term doesn't correspond to the way we use the word *subject* in everyday talk.

As we learned in Chapter 3, this is actually a good thing for writers. It means that the subjects of our clauses don't have to correspond to the thing we're writing about. And that, in turn, means we get to experiment grammatically. As I like to think of it, it makes available all the "colours" of the grammatical spectrum.

The other piece of good news is that our linguistic intuition is completely aligned to the metalinguistic notion of the "subject," which we discover when we remember to use the question-tag probe.

To test this out, have a look at one of the clauses from the first paragraphs of the first chapter of *Alice's Adventures in Wonderland* and ask yourself what the clause is about.

The hot day made her feel very sleepy and stupid

It's about Alice, right? She's the one who feels sleepy and stupid.

Now use a question tag to find the subject.

The hot day made her feel very sleepy and stupid, didn't it?

The pronoun in the question tag is *it*, which already suggests that the subject of the clause isn't Alice. But we don't have to guess. We can do the next step in the process, which is to find out what it is in the clause that *it* refers to.

The secret here is to find the *exact* phrase that the pronoun in the question tag can replace, which in this case, is *the hot day*. You can do something called a replacement test to check your work. Rewrite the clause,

replacing *the hot day* with *it*. Does it work?
Yes.

It *made her feel very sleepy and stupid*

Once you've completed all these steps, and done a replacement test to check your work, you can feel pretty confident that you've found the subject of the clause: *the hot day*.

The hot day is the grammatical subject of the clause, but it's not necessarily what the clause is about. This clause, like almost every other clause in the first paragraph of the book, and indeed, most of the whole book, is about Alice. But did you notice how this way of putting it makes Alice's feelings of sleepiness and stupidity come across not as character traits, but as something that's being done to her by the oppressive weather? Making *the hot day* the subject is one way this effect is achieved.

Writing Prompt: Let's change the subject

Invent a character, and write a short piece of fiction or a poem about them. Have a look at each of your clauses and use the question-tag probe to identify the subject of each. How often does your character show up in the grammatical subject position?

Try rewriting the piece and changing the subjects of most or all of the clauses. You don't have to remove references to your character, just take them away from the grammatical subject role. For instance, you could change <u>Mary</u> *was a fearsome, curmudgeonly creature* to <u>Mary's friends</u> *thought her a fearsome, curmudgeonly creature.* Or even: <u>A steady stream of disappointments</u> *had made Mary a fearsome, curmudgeonly creature.*

Read the original piece and the reworked one. Which do you prefer? What are the different effects produced by each? You may wish to combine clauses from each piece in your final draft.

Misguided assumption 2: The subject can only be so long

You may have been taught in school that the subject of a clause is one word only. If so, your teacher was asking you to find something called the "simple subject." From what I can tell from the online grammar lessons I've scrolled through, the main reason for orienting students to simple subjects is to help them ensure their subjects agree with their verbs.

I'm not a fan of finding the "simple subject" of a clause. I can't think of any reason to reduce the subject to one word except to avoid being grammar shamed for subject-verb agreement errors in your writing. And there's so much more scope for imagining the creative possibilities when we identify the "complete subject," or the *entire noun phrase* that's serving as the subject element of a given clause.

Imagining the creative possibilities is what we're doing this for, isn't it? And the question-tag probe not only makes it easy to do so, it'll also help you and your students spot those moments when your subjects and verbs aren't agreeing with each other, which you'll discover when we get to verbs.

But for now, we'll stick to the subject. And to do so we'll return to Alice, who may be feeling sleepy and stupid in the hot day now, but whose adventure is about to start. In fact, it starts as soon as the final clause of the second paragraph: *suddenly a White Rabbit with pink eyes ran close by her.*

Now, if you're as excited about using the question-tag probe to find the subject as I am, I'm guessing you've skipped ahead. You've found the question tag already:

Suddenly a White Rabbit with pink eyes ran close by her, didn't it?

And then you might have scurried ahead as quickly as our new Rabbit friend, checking your pocket-watch and fearing you'll be late, and used the pronoun *it* to help you find the subject.

When my students rush ahead like this, and I ask them what the subject is, many of them shout out "the Rabbit!"

This level of enthusiasm is exactly what we're going for.

This kind of answer is exactly *not* what we're going for.

The point of finding the subject of a clause is to find *the exact phrase* that's serving as the subject of the clause. If we want to understand how language can create a particular image in our minds, we need to look at the language, not the image.

At this point my slightly subdued student tries again. "A White Rabbit?"

We're getting closer, but we're still not there. There's another step to using the question-tag probe to find the subject that's easy to miss. The pronoun *it* points you in the direction of *a White Rabbit,* but you still need to do the replacement test to see what the subject is in its entirety.

I call this "finding the whole shebang." You'll be able to tell that *a White Rabbit* is not the whole shebang when you replace that bit with *it.*

Suddenly **it** *with pink eyes ran close by her*

Your brain is likely to tell you the clause is a bit off. In this instance, you should listen to your brain, and make it sound better. You'll most likely come up with this:

Suddenly **it** *ran close by her*

See what happened there? Replacing the subject with the subject pronoun *it* shows you that the subject is bigger than you might have initially thought: *a White Rabbit with pink eyes*. The subject is the whole shebang.

Here's how the process works, step by step:
1. Attach a question tag to the end of the clause: *Suddenly a White Rabbit with pink eyes ran close by her*, didn't it?
2. Check to see what the pronoun in the question tag (*it*) refers to: *Suddenly **a White Rabbit with pink eyes** ran close by her,* didn't **it**?
3. Do a replacement test to check your work: *Suddenly* **it** *ran close by her*.
4. If the replacement test works, you've found the subject—it's the whole phrase that the pronoun replaced (the whole shebang): ***a White Rabbit with pink eyes***

What if I get it wrong?

Imagine the scenario: you've set off to find the subject of a clause, you've used the question-tag probe, you've found what the pronoun in the tag refers to, you've located the subject. Or you think you have. But you're so filled with enthusiasm that you omit step three. You forget to do the replacement test, and the subject you identify is not "the whole shebang."

What happens then?

Absolutely nothing bad. You won't be shunned by

your community. You won't be hunted down by the grammar police. You won't be exposed as a fraud. You might hear a voice, maybe mine, maybe your own, asking encouragingly "Is that the whole shebang?" And then maybe you'll go back and change your answer.

Or you won't. The point of using the question-tag probe is that it gives you access to your own linguistic intuition—you don't have to rely on some seemingly arbitrary set of ideas as to what the subject of a clause is. If you discover you haven't located "the whole shebang," you have the tools to go back and fix it.

But you don't have to. The kind of grammar we're playing with in this book is not about always "getting it right." It's about having fun.

And the kind of fun that finding "the whole shebang" offers is that it makes you more aware of creative possibilities. You can write clauses with one-word subjects. You can write clauses with 1000-word subjects. Here's how:

*Suddenly **it** (one word) ran close by her*
*Suddenly **a Rabbit** (two words) ran close by her*
*Suddenly **a White Rabbit** (three words) ran close by her*
*Suddenly **a strange White Rabbit** (four words) ran close by her*
*Suddenly **a surprisingly verbose White Rabbit** (five words) ran close by her*
*Suddenly **a White Rabbit with pink eyes** (six words) ran close by her*
*Suddenly **a loquacious, supercilious-looking White Rabbit who bore a striking resemblance to Alice's Uncle Fred** (loads of words) ran close by her*

There, wasn't that fun? And what's even more fun

is knowing that all the above clauses share the same question tag: *didn't it?* And all the above underlined subjects can be replaced with the pronoun *it*.

Writing Prompt: Adventures in Grammarland

Alice's adventure begins with her falling down a rabbit hole and continues with her consuming questionable foodstuffs that make her alternately shrink and expand. "What a curious feeling!" she says when she downs the contents of a bottle labelled DRINK ME. "I must be shutting up like a telescope." After a few bites of a currant-topped cake marked EAT ME, her telescopic self goes the other direction. "Now I'm opening out like the largest telescope that ever was!" (Then she quite sensibly bids good-bye to her feet.)

If Alice's experience appeals to your own sense of adventure, there are many ways of replicating it, as fans of the band Jefferson Airplane will be aware. If you're looking for an alternative that does not require the use of controlled substances, you can experiment with telescoping the subjects of clauses. You can do this exercise with one of Lewis Carroll's clauses (below), or you can write your own.

The wise little Alice was not going to do that in a hurry

First, use the question-tag probe to find the subject.

<u>The wise little Alice</u> *was not going to do that in a hurry,* was **she**?

Now try telescoping your subject to make it smaller. You've already done that if you used the replacement test:

> **She** *was not going to do that in a hurry*

But you can also experiment with other single-word subjects that aren't pronouns:

> <u>**Alice**</u> *was not going to do that in a hurry*
> <u>**Girlfriend**</u> *was not going to do that in a hurry*

Once you've exhausted all your single-word subjects, move to double-word, triple-word and then loads-of-words subjects. Once you've done "loads of words" you could then challenge yourself to "even more loads of words," *ad infinitum*.

Play around with your expansive creations and see if they're asking to be made into something other than a grammar exercise, perhaps a poem or a playful children's story.

Misguided assumption 3: The subject is the thing that comes first in a clause

Remember how impressed we were when we discovered that my two-year-and-eight-months-old niece was grammatically astute enough to know that the subject comes before the verb? Likely she also knew that to say *Jake take my blocks away!* would function as an accusation, whereas *Take, Jake, my blocks away!* might be heard as an invitation. (Not that he needed an invitation, of course.)

The order of clause elements in languages is regular enough for comparative linguists to be able to classify the world's languages accordingly. English is what's known as an SVO language (subject-verb-object), and it shares that characteristic with other languages such as French, Italian and Swahili. All the other combinations are also possible: Korean and Persian use SOV, Welsh and Classical Arabic use VSO, Fijian and Malagasy use VOS. OVS and OSV structures are much rarer, but still can be found in certain languages.

I find this kind of thing fascinating, to the extent that I've sometimes forced students to identify the clause structures of unknown languages using just a few clues. We won't be doing that here. Nor will we be worrying too much about the fact that the word "object" is used in linguistic typology, while we'll be using the word "complement" in this book. (Or, at least, I hope you're not worrying about that. If you are, skip ahead to Chapter 8 for reassurance.)

The other thing we're not going to do is to fall into the trap of assuming that the subject is always going to be the first thing in an English clause, just because English is an SVO-structured language. The beauty of language structure, as I hope you're discovering, is that it allows us to experiment, to change things up, to play. *Most of the time* the subject comes before the verb in an English clause. But it's not necessarily the first thing, as we discovered when we used the question-tag probe on *suddenly a White Rabbit with pink eyes ran close by her.* The first thing in that clause, *suddenly*, is a different clause element entirely (the adjunct, which you'll learn about in Chapter 9).

Of course, in the White Rabbit clause, the subject still adheres to the SVO structure in that the subject comes before the verb. But there are plenty of instances in which the verb comes before the subject. Questions are a perfect example. In fact, question *tags* are the quintessential example, where the verb (the auxiliary) comes before the subject pronoun. Doesn't it?

Questions aside, sometimes speakers and writers will change the subject-verb order around for literary effect. Here's an example from *Alice's Adventures*.

Round the neck of the bottle was a paper label

Sometimes my students get flummoxed by sentences like these, because they're inclined to look to the beginning of the clause to find the subject. They might be tempted to say *the bottle* is the subject, or *the neck of the bottle* or *round the neck of the bottle*.

But ultimately they don't say any of these things because they've learned how to use the question-tag probe, which, like a trusty sniffer-dog will find the subject almost anywhere you hide it. Let's give it a try.

Round the neck of the bottle was a paper label, wasn't **it**?

Now all we have to do is recognise that *it* refers to *a paper label*, and then check by doing a replacement test.

Round the neck of the bottle was **it**

Now, that might sound a little strange. Your brain might want to try to correct it to something like *Round the neck of the bottle* **it** *was* (if you're channelling Yoda) or **It** *was round the neck of the bottle*. Once again, trust your linguistic intuition, which is just trying to shift the clause into a more recognisable, more English-sounding structure. The point is that the thing that *it* replaces, *a paper label,* is indeed the subject of the clause. Good brain!

Misguided assumption 4: The subject will be a concrete noun or noun phrase

You may have been taught at some point in your grammatical education that subjects are noun phrases.

Congratulations on learning that! It's totally true. You're a step ahead of the game.

But knowing that subjects are noun phrases sometimes pulls up a bunch of other misguided assumptions about what nouns are, and what noun phrases look like. You might not have realised that noun phrases can have lots of other phrases embedded in them. Sometimes one or more whole clauses will sneak their way into a noun phrase. Also, labelling words like *pencil*, *table*, *cup* and *book* as nouns might have gotten you into the habit of assuming that nouns are always "concrete"—objects you can point to, touch or buy on Amazon. Certainly you've *heard* of abstract nouns, but they might not be the first things that pop into your head when you're in noun-spotting mode.

Enter another reason I'm in love with the question-tag probe. The pronoun in the question tag (indeed, pronouns in general) will reliably point you in the direction of noun phrases, regardless of how nouny or un-nouny these phrases might seem on first glance.

Try it with me with another clause from *Alice's Adventures*: *the pleasure of making a daisy-chain would be worth the trouble of getting up and picking the daisies*. This time, see if you can find the subject without using the question-tag probe.

Now use the question-tag probe and see what it brings.

The pleasure of making a daisy-chain would be worth the trouble of getting up and picking the daisies, wouldn't **it**?

What does *it* replace in the above clause?

If you came up with *the pleasure of making a daisy-chain*, count yourself correct. Or better yet, double check it with the replacement test.

It *would be worth the trouble of getting up and picking the daisies.*

Bingo!

Does it matter that *the pleasure of making a daisy-chain* might not seem particularly nouny, or that you can't buy such a thing on Amazon? No, it doesn't matter. Not one bit. We can have faith in the question-tag probe. (Except when we can't, but really, there are only a very few times when we can't.)

> ### Writing prompt: Maybe you *can* buy it on Amazon
>
> Write a poem, blog or twitter thread entitled "the pleasure of making a daisy-chain."

Misguided assumption 4: DRINK ME

Remember the label that was round the neck of the bottle in Alice's adventure? You may remember from the story that the label says DRINK ME. You'll also know that "the wise little Alice was not going to do *that* in a hurry." Was she? (Sorry, it's becoming something of a habit.)

The rest of that part of the book tells us that Alice was savvy enough to check whether the bottle was marked "poison" before she followed the label's instructions. Finding no such label, she guzzled it down.

We're not here to judge Alice's misguided assumptions, though, but to root out any we might still have about finding the subject of a clause. And one misguided assumption might be that you can't use the question-tag probe to find the subject of a clause like *Drink me.*

The grammatically learned among you may recognise

the clause *Drink me* as an imperative. You may remember learning that imperatives have an implied (or understood) subject.

If you don't know what the secret unspoken subject of an imperative is, you don't have to worry. You've been given a special decoder ring, better known as the question-tag probe, that will take you straight there. Just stick a question tag at the end of the clause *Drink me*.

Did you get something like *Drink me, won't you?* Or *Drink me, will you?*

Either way, the question tag has reliably revealed the hidden subject of an imperative clause: *you*.

Please agree with me that that's the coolest thing ever. Won't you?

Sorry.

Impressed with the question-tag probe?

Are you excited by all the ways it will help you and your students find the subject? Are you already dreaming up ways the question-tag probe will make writing feel more like play and less like a chore?

Me too. But we've only just begun. The question-tag probe can tell us so much more about a clause than just what the subject is. Stay tuned to find out more.

Exercise: Stumped on the subject?

I've discovered in my undergraduate teaching that the sense of empowerment students feel when they first use the question-tag probe can quickly turn to disappointment when they run into trickier clauses. I use a strategy called "Stump your classmates" to try to preempt that disappointment. I ask the students to write clauses that are specifically designed to make it hard on their peers. (Often their clauses end up stumping me as well, which does wonders for my humility.)

Here are some of the ones they came up with in a "finding the subject" exercise. Use the question-tag probe to find the subject of each clause, and try not to be stumped.
1. Not sleeping the night before your 9 a.m. seminar isn't a smart decision
2. Often it's difficult to power through a lecture with no caffeine or happiness
3. This girl that I was talking to at the bus stop told me that my clothes didn't match
4. Lots of Lucy's dolls have personalities
5. Sometimes destroying your emotional wellbeing for the sake of finishing your assignment is not well advised

5 VERB VIBES

Do verbs make you tense?

An early iteration of my Refreshing Grammar course[23] had a unit called "Do verbs make you tense?" I'd posed it as a rhetorical question, but several of the participants responded to it anyway, strongly in the affirmative: VERBS MAKE ME VERY TENSE.

If you're a teacher, you'll know exactly what they mean. In primary school kids often learn that verbs are "doing words," and if they're lucky they get to embody this concept by dancing, skipping, jumping and verbing all over the classroom. But verbing in secondary school is an entirely different matter. Students start reading Dickens, for goodness' sake, and encounter prose like this:

> Oh! But he was a tight-fisted hand at the grindstone, Scrooge! a squeezing, wrenching, grasping, scraping, clutching, covetous, old sinner![24]

There's nothing stopping you from getting your 14-year-olds to embody the verbs in this passage—if they haven't already sauntered across the too-cool-for-school threshold, that is. You could invite them to move about the classroom dramatically, trying their hands (and the rest of their bodies) at squeezing, wrenching, grasping, scraping, clutching and covetousing...

Covetousing?

Covetous isn't a verb.

Neither is *old*, come to think of it.

So what are *covetous* and *old* doing in a list of words that look (and feel) like verbs?

Wait. What actually *is* a verb?

This is the kind of question that could trigger a panic attack, especially if you ask it of yourself in the middle of a teaching session. Even more so if a student asks it of you.

You're the teacher, right? You're supposed to know this stuff.

And I happen to know it's not just teachers who get nervous about verbs. Writers, have you ever felt that sinking anxiety that accompanies an editor remarking on "inconsistent tense?" Like, what are they asking you to *do* about that? Even my linguist colleagues sometimes confess to being unsure about the difference between tense and aspect. These worries form part of something I affectionally call "advanced level grammar shaming," and I'm imploring you not to sign up to it.

Remember how enjoyable and empowering it was to locate the subject of a clause using the question-tag probe?

What if I told you that the same probe can be used to find the verb element of a clause?

It can also help you "solve" that tense inconsistency thing your editor insists on taking issue with. Even better, it can embolden you to use tense shifting to your creative advantage.

Let's give it a try.

Using question tags to find verbs

You haven't forgotten how to use the question-tag probe, have you? (Sorry.) In case you need a refresher, have a go at adding a question tag to the end of each of the following clauses.
1. I am not answering my phone
2. My boss has been ringing all day
3. She is asking me to cover for Ollie again
4. But I covered Ollie's shift yesterday
5. So she can forget about me doing it today

There, that was easy, wasn't it? (Not sorry.) If all the stuff about Dickens, tenses and verbs stressed you out, now's the time to have a look at the answers below and revel in how smart the three-year-old inside your brain is.
1. I am not answering my phone, *am I?*
2. My boss has been ringing all day, *hasn't she?*
3. She is asking me to cover for Ollie again, *isn't she?*
4. But I covered Ollie's shift yesterday, *didn't I?*
5. So she can forget about me doing it today, *can't she?*

And while you're soaking up the endorphin rush of having found the right answers, why not take it to the next level and find the subjects of the above clauses? (In case you need a reminder, just look to the pronouns in the question tags and see what they're referring to.)

The answers are below. (The subjects are **underlined and in bold**. The pronouns in the question tags are in **bold**.)
1. <u>**I**</u> am not answering my phone, *am **I**?*
2. <u>**My boss**</u> has been ringing all day, *hasn't **she**?*

3. **She** is asking me to cover for Ollie again, *isn't she?*
4. But **I** covered Ollie's shift yesterday, *didn't I?*
5. So **she** can forget about me doing it today, *can't she?*

If you want to reward yourself with a cookie, you'll not hear any objections from me.

And now, gentle reader, we're going to have a look at the verb elements of these clauses. And when I say *we*, I mean, *me*. I'm going to tell you what the verb elements are while you eat another cookie.

I've underlined them below. (The verb elements, not the cookies.)

1. I **am not answering** my phone, *am I?*
2. My boss **has been ringing** all day, *hasn't she?*
3. She **is asking** me to cover for Ollie again, *isn't she?*
4. But I **covered** Ollie's shift yesterday, *didn't I?*
5. So she **can forget** about me doing it today, *can't she?*

There's a couple of things about the verbs I've underlined that might have spiked your anxiety again, so let's just address these before we move on to the fun part. You might be wondering about other verbs in the above clauses, like *to cover* in 3 or *doing* in 5. You might not have thought that finding verbs meant finding more than one word, which was the case in every clause but 4. And you might not have included the *not* in clause 1.

These are all valid, eagle-eyed questions. We'll get to each of them, I promise. But for now can I ask you to have a look at something fascinating? Check out the first word of the verb element in most of the above clauses… and compare them with the first word in their associated

question tags.
   1. I ***am* not answering** my phone, ***am** I*?
   2. My boss ***has* been ringing** all day, ***hasn't** she?*
   3. She ***is* asking** me to cover for Ollie again, ***isn't** she?*
   5. So she ***can* forget** about me doing it today, ***can't** she?*

Is it a coincidence that these are the exact same words? I think not. I know not, in fact. You may remember from Chapter 3 that question tags are composed of two words: an auxiliary and a subject pronoun. (Most of the time you'll also find the reduced negative particle, *n't*, attached to the auxiliary.) The auxiliary your brain produces when you ask it for a question tag is never random. It will always be the first auxiliary in the verb element of a clause (except sometimes for verbs in the simple aspect, which you'll learn about soon).[25]

Finding the verb element of a clause

What actually is that little word at the beginning of the question tag, and why does it carry so much power? I've mentioned that it's called an *auxiliary*, which is a type of verb. *Auxiliary* comes from the Latin *auxilium*, which means "help." Indeed, when I was a kid I was taught to call them *helping verbs*. They were supposed to "help" the main verb of a clause, which is also called the *lexical verb*, which is the type of verb you might have been taught was a "doing word." (I call the lexical verbs "verby verbs," which I realise is overwhelmingly unhelpful, but I don't care because lexical verbs aren't supposed to be helpful. That's what helping verbs are for.)

Before we get swept away, like Alice, in a flood of our

own grammar-induced tears, let's start with some basic principles. The verb element of a clause consists of one or more of the following parts: auxiliaries, lexical verbs and negative particles (*not* or *n't*). They can have more than one auxiliary. They have only one[26] lexical verb.[27]

With this in mind, let's go through the process of using the question-tag probe to find the verb element of a clause. We'll start with one we already know the answer to.

She is asking me to cover for Ollie again, isn't she?

The first step is to locate the auxiliary in the question tag, which is easy peasy lemon squeezy. It's the first thing in the tag before the *n't*. In this case, *is*.

The next step is to check for that exact auxiliary in the clause itself. In this case we're looking for the word *is*, which we can spot right away.

*She **is** asking me to cover for Ollie again,* **is**n't she?

Now we're on the scent! The auxiliary that shows up in the question tag points to the first part of the verb element. To find the rest of the verb element, we just keep looking to the right. What are we looking for? First we look for *not* or *n't*, then we look for any other auxiliaries, then we look for the lexical verb. Once we get to the lexical verb, we stop.

OK, so there's no *not* or *n't* in the clause we're looking at—that's easy enough. The word that comes after *is* is *asking*. How are you supposed to know if it's an auxiliary or a lexical verb (or something else entirely)?

Well, I've got good news and bad news in response to that excellent question. The good news is that there is a very limited number of auxiliaries in English. The primary auxiliaries are all forms of *do, be* and *have*. The modal auxiliaries are *can, could, shall, should, will, would, may, might* and *must*. So you don't have to spend a lot of time worrying about whether a word is an auxiliary. You can just check it against the words I just listed. (More on auxiliaries in Chapter 7.)

The bad news is that you can't just assume that if it's not an auxiliary than it must be a lexical verb. This is because sometimes other clause elements (notably, adjuncts) like to wheedle their way into verb elements. If verb elements were in therapy, they'd be told they have boundary issues.

So let's look at our example clause again. We've found the first part of the verb element with *is*, so let's look to the next word: *asking*.

She **is asking** me to cover for Ollie again.

We know *asking* isn't an auxiliary, because we can check it against our list of primary and modal auxiliaries. (You don't have to systematically check every time—it's OK just to know.) Is it a lexical verb?

Spoiler alert: yes.

But how can we know for sure it's a lexical verb?

Annoying answer alert: because it feels verby.

You might want me to justify this response, using some impressive sounding metalinguistic terminology, but do you know what I mean when I say it feels verby? Does the three-year-old in your brain know what I mean?

I mean it feels like a doing word. It's something you could act out with reasonable success in a game of charades. (I myself would position my shoulders and arms in an "asking" sort of pose, then put my hand to my ear as if anticipating an answer.) It means you could do a version of that annoying rhyme about ice cream: *I scream, you scream, we all scream for ice cream!* (*I ask, you ask, we all ask...*) It means you can put verby suffixes on the end of it, like *-ing* and *-ed*: I'm *asking* for ice cream, I *asked* for ice cream, etc.

It might be helpful at this point to see what it looks like when the word following the auxiliary isn't a lexical verb. Try this version of the clause.

> She **is undoubtably** asking me to cover for Ollie again.

This time when we look to the right of *is*, we find *undoubtably*. Does *undoubtably* feel verby? *I undoubtably, you undoubtably, we all undoubtably for ice cream? I am undoubtablying, you undoubtabled?* Even just typing those expressions is making my spelling and grammar checkers flare up in red squiggly lines.

Like the grammar bots that live in my word processor, your brain can tell the difference between lexical verbs and other types of word.

If on your treasure hunt for the verb element of a clause, you come across a word that isn't an auxiliary, *not/n't* or a lexical verb, leave it out. It's an interloper, and we'll deal with it later. When you get to the lexical verb, stop there. The phrase you end up with is your verb element.

So the verb element in *She is asking me to cover for Ollie again* is ***is asking***.

And the verb element in *She is undoubtably asking me to cover for Ollie again* is also ***is asking***.

Do, do, do

Now do you understand (even more) why I'm so obsessed with the question-tag probe? It not only helps us find the subject, but it reliably points us in the direction of the verb element of a clause.

If in a fit of excited glee, you've applied the process for finding the verb to the clauses introduced at the beginning of the chapter, you might have come across a snag.

Isn't there always a snag? Actually, the snag we're going to address now is a pretty cool one. It has to do with when a form of the word *do* (*do, does* or *did*) shows up in the question tag, as in:

But I covered Ollie's shift yesterday, **did**n't I?

Having successfully identified the auxiliary in the question tag *(did)*, you then go on to find its twin in the clause itself. And then... snag city.

There's no *did*. What's a verb tracker to do?

When I was first developing the method of using M. A. K. Halliday's mood tags to find the verb element in a clause, hitting this particular snag resulted in a eureka moment. I learned that in clauses where the question-tag probe produces a *do* auxiliary, the aspect of the verb was always *simple*. (*Do* and *does* indicate that the tense-aspect combination is present simple. *Did* indicates past simple.)[28]

We'll go into tense and aspect in more detail in Chapter 7, but for now I'll just say one thing about verb in the simple aspect in English. This is the only aspect where you get to choose whether you want to use the auxiliary or not. So you can say *covered* or *did cover*, as the following clauses show.

*But I **covered** Ollie's shift yesterday,* **did**n't I?
*But I **did cover** Ollie's shift yesterday,* **did**n't I?

Note that for both, the question tag is the same.

Are there reasons for including the *do-does-did* auxiliary for a clause in the simple aspect? Sure. Maybe you want to emphasise the verb: *I really did cover Ollie's shift, honest I did!* Maybe you want to put it in the negative (*I didn't cover Ollie's shift*) without sounding like you're addressing an Elizabethan noble *(I covered not Ollie's shift, my Lord)*. Maybe you need to ask a question: *Did I cover Ollie's shift?*

But apart from adding emphasis and forming negatives and questions, most of the time you'll keep verbs in the simple aspect, well, simple. You'll use the lexical verb with no auxiliary *(covered)*.

The thing to keep in mind at this point is that when you come across *do, does* or *did* in your question-tag probe, you might not find these words in your clause. That means you can't use the auxiliary as your starting point for finding the verb element. What should you do?

My favourite hack is to simply insert the auxiliary in the question tag into the clause and rewrite it accordingly. Here's what I mean.

*But I **covered** Ollie's shift yesterday,* **did**n't I?
becomes
*But I **did cover** Ollie's shift yesterday*

And then it becomes clear that *did cover* means pretty much the same thing as *covered*, and therefore *covered* is the verb element.

Finding the verb element in steps

Using the question-tag probe to find the verb element of a clause requires a little more work, and a few more steps, than finding the subject. But it's worth doing because it packs a big punch. The question-tag probe can give us all sorts of assistance with advanced-level grammar questions, like distinguishing between finite and non-finite verbs, identifying the tense and aspect of a verb, determining the modality of a clause, etc. We'll learn about all of these in the next two chapters. For now, it's enough just to learn the following steps for finding the verb. And if you don't feel like memorising them, just bookmark this section and return to it as needed!

1. Add a question tag to the clause.
2. Find the auxiliary in the tag.
3. Look for the auxiliary in the clause. (If the auxiliary in the tag is *do, does,* or *did,* be aware that you might not find it in the clause. If that's the case, look for the single lexical verb in the clause that could be rewritten with a *do* auxiliary, and stop there.)
4. Look immediately to the right of the auxiliary in the clause.
5. Is it a negative particle (*not* or *n't*)? If so, include it as part of the verb element.
6. Look to the next word on the right. Is it another auxiliary? (Remember, the primary auxiliaries are forms of *do, be* or *have,* and the modal auxiliaries are *can, could, shall, should, will, would, may, might* and *must.*) If so, include it as part of the verb element and keeping going until you get to the lexical verb.
7. If you come across a word that's not an auxiliary or a lexical verb, leave it out and keep going until you get to the lexical verb.
8. When you get to the lexical verb, stop there. Write it down at the end of your string of words.

You've found the verb element of the clause. Have another cookie.

Verb elements in the wild

Before I set you loose on looking for verb elements in the lyrics of your favourite songs, the lines from your favourite poems and the text messages of your favourite loved ones, shall we have a look at a few potentially tricky ones together? I've taken a few clauses from Zadie Smith's novel, *White Teeth*,[29] to prepare you for what verb elements look like when they haven't been carefully constructed by your favourite grammar book writer.

I'll list them for you all at once if you'd like to have a go first before I talk you through the answers.

1. Their wartime friendship had been severed by thirty years of separation across continents
2. He wanted it to be perfectly quiet and still, like the inside of an empty confessional box or the moment in the brain between thought and speech
3. Every school has one
4. He wasn't the type to make elaborate plans
5. Once upon a time he had been a track cyclist
6. Like you've just been handed a great big wad of Time

I'm sure you've already started on step one for all of them —adding a question tag to the end of each of the clauses. You may have even overachieved and found the subjects. Below the question tags are in *italics* and the subjects of the clauses are **<u>underlined and in bold</u>**.

1. **<u>Their wartime friendship</u>** had been severed by thirty years of separation across continents,

hadn't it?
2. **He** wanted it to be perfectly quiet and still, like the inside of an empty confessional box or the moment in the brain between thought and speech, *didn't he?*
3. **Every school** has one, *doesn't it?*
4. **He** wasn't the type to make elaborate plans, *was he?*
5. Once upon a time **he** had been a track cyclist, *hadn't he?*
6. Like **you**'ve just been handed a great big wad of Time, *haven't you?*

Are you still with me? Great. Now let's start tracking some verb elements.

Clause 1 is pretty straightforward. We look to the auxiliary in the question tag, *had*, and find its twin in the clause itself. So far so good.

1. Their wartime friendship **had** been severed by thirty years of separation across continents, *hadn't it?*

Now we look to the right of *had* and find the word *been*. What kind of word is *been*? Well, it's a form of the auxiliary *be*. (The other forms are *am, is, are, was, were* and *being*.) We've learned that verb elements can have more than one auxiliary, so we can go ahead and underline it.

*Their wartime friendship **had been** severed by thirty years of separation across continents*

We're still on the hunt for a lexical verb, so we look to the right of *been* to find *severed*. How verby is *severed*? Pretty verby. It's got that -ed ending, for one. You could act it out pretty well in a game of charades. (I'd probably mimic severing my own head.) And you can shout *I sever, you sever, we all sever (heads) for ice cream!* Which would be a morbid thing to shout, but grammatically it works. So underline away.

> *Their wartime friendship **had been severed** by thirty years of separation across continents*

Once we get to the lexical verb, we stop (and eat a cookie). The verb element for the above clause is *had been severed*.

Does that feel good? Great! Let's move on to the next one.

> 2. He wanted it to be perfectly quiet and still, like the inside of an empty confessional box or the moment in the brain between thought and speech, *didn't he?*

Here we have a situation where a *do* verb *(did)* has shown up in the question tag. We'll look for *did* in the clause, but we know better than to be disappointed if it doesn't show up.

Sure enough, it's not there. So we look to see where you could put *did* in the clause.

> *He ~~wanted~~ **did want** it to be perfectly quiet and still, like the inside of an empty confessional box or the moment in the brain between thought and speech,* didn't he?

Since *did want* means pretty much the same thing as *wanted*, we can be assured that *wanted* is the lexical verb that the question-tag probe is pointing to. And since *wanted* is a lexical verb, we stop there.

> *He **wanted** it to be perfectly quiet and still, like the inside of an empty confessional box or the moment in the brain between thought and speech*

Wanted is the verb element of the above clause. A long

clause can have a one-word verb element. That's fine by us. Let's try a short clause now.

    3. Every school has one, *doesn't it?*

Another *do* auxiliary—*does*—and we know exactly what to, ahem, do. Since there's no *does* in the clause, we look to where *does* would go.

    Every school ~~has~~ ***does have*** *one,* doesn't it?

Does have means pretty much the same thing as *has*, right? Which means that *has* is the lexical verb that the question-tag probe is pointing to, and the verb element is *has*.

Hold on a cotton-pickin' second, I hear you say. *Isn't* has *a form of* have? *And isn't* have *on the list of primary auxiliaries, along with forms of* do *and* be?

So I guess now is the right time to tell you that the three primary auxiliaries—*do, be* and *have*—can also function as lexical verbs. Lexical verbs are often understood as having content, or meaning, as opposed to auxiliaries, which have grammatical function but not a lot of meaning. So when *do* means something like *act*, when *be* means something like *exist* and when *have* means something like *possess*—in these instances they're lexical verbs. Isn't language ~~annoying~~ **fascinating**?

In the next clause we'll see an instance in which *be* acts as a lexical verb.

    4. He wasn't the type to make elaborate plans, *was he?*

You're probably getting so good at this right now that the steps are blurring together a little. By now you've probably already found the auxiliary in the question tag (*was*) and matched it to its twin in the clause.

He ***was****n't the type to make elaborate plans,* was he?

Now you're dutifully looking to the right—and what do you see but a negative particle? Perfect! You know by now to include this as part of your verb element.

> He **wasn't** the type to make elaborate plans

And you keep looking to the right to look for your lexical verb. And you find *the, type* and *to*. None of these seem particularly verby, so you keep going. And you find *make*.

Perfect, you think. You've followed all the steps, you've landed on the lexical verb, you can write down your verb element with confidence. *Wasn't make.*

What?!

If the three-year-old inside your brain is telling you that *wasn't make* doesn't feel like a well formed verb element, you should listen. Just because you have a set of steps to follow from your trusty book on grammar doesn't mean you should override your linguistic intuition. That part of you knows that *wasn't making* feels like a verb element and *wasn't made* works too, but not *wasn't make*.

But isn't *make a lexical verb?* I hear you protesting. I can see you acting it out in an impromptu game of charades, pressing your hands together to mime forming bricks out of clay. *I make, you make, we all make ice cream!* I hear you scream.

OK, OK. I get it. No need to shout.

Yes, *make* is a lexical verb. But it's not part of the verb element of this clause. Verb elements in finite clauses are finite verbs, and *make* (in this clause) is non-finite.

And I know you're desperate to learn the difference between finite and non-finite verbs, and I promise we'll go over it in Chapter 6, but for now trust me when I tell you that the question-tag probe points to the finite verb in a finite clause.

So what happened in this clause?

It turns out that *wasn't* is the finite verb here. *Wasn't* on its own. It's functioning as a lexical verb, better known as a copular verb. I know it doesn't feel particularly verby, but it does actually work with the ice cream chant: *I wasn't, you weren't, we all weren't ice cream!*

Forms of *be* show up pretty frequently in the wild as verb elements *(am, are, is, was, were)*, so it's probably worth being prepared for that. In fact, we'll see another example of it with clause 5.

5. Once upon a time he had been a track cyclist, hadn't he?

By now you know the drill. Find the auxiliary in the question tag, *had*, look for its twin in the clause, underline it and then look to the right. *Been. Been*, we know now, is a form of *be*, which can be either an auxiliary or a lexical verb. Either way, it's part of the verb element, so let's get underlining.

*Once upon a time he **had been** a track cyclist*

Now all we have to do is check for another lexical verb... which we don't find. So we can be pretty sure *had been* is the verb element. *(I had been, you had been, we all had been ice cream!)*

The only reason I'm labouring the point about the *be* verbs (otherwise known as the copular verbs) is that they so often perplex my students. *Be* and its forms just don't feel like doing verbs. Because, strictly speaking, they're not. They're *being* verbs. Maybe it's the pressures of capitalist culture that trick us into thinking that verbs have to be doing productive stuff all the time. Why can't verbs sometimes just... be?

You're so well initiated into the process for finding finite verb elements by now that clause 6 is going to be a breeze. There are a couple of potential snags in this one, but these aren't going to faze you, not in the slightest.

    6. Like you've just been handed a great big wad of Time, *haven't you?*

You've spotted the auxiliary in the question tag, and you're looking for its twin. OK, so you don't find *have* in the clause, but you do find its reduced, or contracted form, *'ve*, and you decide that will do just fine. You're 100% correct. I hope you have some cookies left.

Now you're looking to the right, and you find the word *just*. All your tests for lexical verbiness fail, so you reject it. You and the three-year-old in your brain know perfectly well that *just* isn't a lexical verb. Nobody ever *justed* for ice cream.

Once more to the right, and you find the word *been*, which doesn't daunt you in the slightest. *Been* could be either an auxiliary or a lexical verb. You know you don't have to figure out which one it is yet, just underline it and move on.

*Like you'**ve** just **been** handed a great big wad of Time*

Next you come upon *handed*. Does it feel verby? If you said yes, then I'm handing you an ice cream cone (with cookies in it). You've found your lexical verb. Underline it, stop there, and admire your work.

*Like you'**ve** just **been handed** a great big wad of Time*

The verb element in clause 6 is *'ve been handed*, or *have been handed* ('cause *'ve* is kind of hard to say).

If you've made it to the end of this chapter and indulged me by going through all the examples step by step, I applaud you. I appreciate you spending your great big wad of Time on working with the question-tag probe. I also appreciate that you won't always need to use every step in the process every time you decide you want to locate the subject and verb of a clause. You may get so good at spotting them (if you're not already) that your inner three-year-old will take over and you won't have to rely upon the steps.

In the spirit of full disclosure, I myself don't go through all the steps to find the subject and the verb. But I still like to use the question-tag probe to check my work... and just to delight in how well the probe works.

Even more importantly, I love how well the probe works to create a sense of empowerment in the classroom. The probe gives my students a way to access certain aspects of grammar that they might not have had access to before. It also gives them a way to help each other figure it out, which creates that supportive, admiring-each-other's-work environment I'm always trying to create.

It might not be the *exact* art room vibe I'm striving for, but it's pretty close.

If you're a teacher, you know what I mean. If you're a writer, chances are you also do some teaching, and so you know what I mean. If you're a writer who doesn't do any teaching, stay with me. In Chapter 6 we are going to use what we've learned about verb elements to have some serious writing fun.

Exercise: Give me a sentence, any sentence

In my teaching career I've often found myself in the desperate position of needing a clause to illustrate a grammatical principle. When I've run out of juice inventing examples, I sometimes ask students in a seminar to "give me a sentence, any sentence."

It turns out that nothing blocks creativity more than being required to produce a string of meaningful words on command.

I've spent a lot of time wondering why this is so, and I've discovered that the brain freezes when the possibilities are unlimited. (I have no scientific research to back this hypothesis, you'll be unsurprised to know.) "Give me a sentence" calls to mind the bewildering infinity of sentences that anyone could produce at any given moment.

The creativity returns, I've discovered, when you impose a constraint, like "give me a sentence where most of the letters start with b," or "where most of the words rhyme" or "where all the words have only one syllable." It's like the brain is now being invited to solve a fun puzzle.

Here are some of the clauses my students have produced over the years when I asked them for clauses where most of the words start with ch or j. Enjoy them! Create some of your own! But first, use the question-tag probe to find the verb elements.

1. Jay has been chanting about choosing cheese
2. The other children will not join the cheese chant
3. Charlie the Chosen Champion of Chile is charging chivalrously into combat
4. The juicy chameleon was choking jubilantly on just one chargrilled chicken nugget
5. The Cheesy Chimpanzees must have been jamming justifiably to Jazzman
6. Charlie and Jill are joyfully jumping

6 NON-FINITE RESOURCES

Getting back in the zone

I'm hoping you're feeling very confident by now about your ability to locate the two essential elements of a clause: the subject and the verb. But such confidence may have come at a price. One participant in the Refreshing Grammar course[29] revealed that she practised using the question-tag probe so much she was no longer capable of reading or hearing a sentence without sticking *isn't it?* or *aren't they?* or *can't she?* at the end of it. If you're facing a similar affliction, I hope all this questioning is happening within the private space of your own mind. I'd hate for people to start doubting your sanity.

The other potential problem with all this locating of subjects and verbs is that it's one of those step-by-step processes that can take you out of your zone of creativity. In this chapter we'll be looking even further into what question tags can tell us about verbs. But can I encourage you to get into a bit more of a creative space when you do it? Maybe return to the coffee shop, or the home office with child-repelling signage, or the art room, if you're lucky enough to have one. Go ahead and light your candle. Pull out the fancy notebook and that pen you like. Take a sip of your favourite brew. I'll wait.

Are you there? OK, how about a nice writing prompt?

Writing prompt: A nice one

> Write the introductory lines of a story, essay or poem about the oppressive stagnancy and inhumanity of bureaucratic institutions.

Wait, what? Am I really proposing to help you break free from the oppression of step-by-step grammar instructions by asking you to write about the oppression of bureaucracy?

Did I just see your jasmine-scented candle flicker in protest?

There is a method to my madness, I promise. My intention here is to illustrate how an understanding of verbs can help you craft pieces on topics like stagnancy, oppression and inhumanity without your style becoming, well... stagnant, oppressive or (inhumanely) boring.

Here's the piece I had in mind when I wrote the prompt:

> *Fog on the Essex marshes, fog on the Kentish heights. Fog creeping into the cabooses of collier-brigs; fog lying out on the yards and hovering in the rigging of great ships; fog drooping on the gunwales of barges and small boats.*

Extra cookies to anyone who recognises this passage from early on in Dickens's *Bleak House*.[30] The novel's about the oppressive stagnancy and inhumanity of bureaucratic institutions (specifically, the English Law Courts, or Chancery), and to my mind this description of the

London fog sets the scene beautifully.

There's more going on here than just the fog imagery, though—something fascinating that's happening at the level of grammar, and we now have the tools to spot it. It has to do with the way the clauses are structured, specifically the verbs.

Clause structure? I hear you say. *Let's get going with some question-tag probes*, I hear you say.

Thumbs up to your enthusiasm. Let's give it a try with the first bit.

Fog on the Essex marshes

Wait, question tags are supposed to be easy, aren't they? (See?) Why is it so hard to find the question tag for this one?

The best I can come up with is *isn't there?* or *wasn't there?* which would work if the clause was one of the following:

There is fog on the Essex marshes, isn't there?
There was fog on the Essex marshes, wasn't there?

The subject of both of these clauses is *there*.[31] The verb in the first one is *is*, and in the second it's *was*.

But that's not what Dickens wrote. He chose *Fog on the Essex marshes*, which, as it turns out, isn't a clause at all. Neither is *fog on the Kentish heights*. If young Charlie had written these lines for an English assignment, he'd probably have had to face the inevitable judgment inscribed in an angry red pen: *These are not complete sentences!*[32]

But we're not doing grammar shaming here, so we'll let him get away with it. For now. The next clause (yes, this one is a clause) looks a bit more promising. Let's have a look:

Fog creeping into the cabooses of collier-brigs

Did you find a question tag? (If it were me, I'd be trying to sneak a peek at my neighbour's work at this point.)

I want to say *isn't it*?

Did you go for *wasn't it*?

Which one's right? Why is there more than one answer? Isn't this supposed to be intuitive and easy?

Top tip: if you or your students are ever analysing a clause "in the wild" and stumble when you're looking for the question tag, don't assume there's something wrong with your linguistic intuition! You're being given very good information about the structure of the clause, as we'll see in a moment.

For now let's test the clause with the question tag *isn't it?* and see how far we get. Let's see if it brings us the subject. Yes, that seems easy enough:

Fog *creeping into the cabooses of collier-brigs,* isn't **it**?

The pronoun in the question tag, *it*, points unproblematically to the noun phrase *fog,* so we seem to be on to a winner there. But when we look to the auxiliary in the tag, *is*, we run into a snag. There's no *is* in the clause. We can see where *is* should go, though, which is just before the lexical verb *creeping*.

If there were an *is* in the clause, the finite verb element would be *is creeping*.

Similarly, if there were a *was* in the clause, the finite verb element would be *was creeping*.

But there's no *is* and no *was*, which tells us that this isn't a finite clause, and that creeping isn't a finite verb.

What is it, then?

To non-finite... and beyond

It's a non-finite clause, with a non-finite verb.

Now's the moment (are you excited?) when you learn the difference between a finite and a non-finite clause.

Finite clauses contain (at the minimum) a subject and a finite verb. A finite verb is marked for tense[33] and agrees with the subject.

Non-finite clauses contain (at the minimum) a non-finite verb, but not necessarily a subject. A non-finite verb is not marked for tense and does not agree with the subject.

Non-finite clauses can worm their way into finite clauses, as you may have noticed with the Eudora Welty piece we studied in Chapter 3.

and, backing against the door, pushed it closed with her hip

There are (count 'em!) three verbs in that clause, one finite and two non-finite. Have you found them yet? *Backing*, *pushed* and *closed*.

How do you know which ones are the finite verbs? Well, you could use the definitions about finite and non-finite verbs I gave above. You could check to see which of the verbs are marked for tense and whether they agree with their subjects.

Hot take: this method is the route to frustration. Let me tell you why.

First, it requires you to find all the verbs in a clause. That should be easy enough, right? Maybe, if you're really good at verb spotting. But verbs can be elusive things, and as you know by now, I'm not a big fan of word-class labelling anyway. I always seem to miss one or two. In my first draft of this section I missed *closed*. Did you miss any?

Second, deciding if something is "marked for tense" is not as easy as people think. Take the word *backing*. When I ask people to tell me the tense of a verb with an *-ing* ending, most of the time they tell me it's the present. Maybe they say that because *-ing* makes it feel like the verb is verbing in the now. Maybe they say it because they're familiar with the term *present participle*, which is another word for verbs ending in *-ing*, except when the verb is a gerund.

I don't know about you, but all this terminology about tense is making me... tense.

As it happens, it was a trick question. (Sorry.) Verbs ending in *-ing* aren't actually marked for tense. When they're on their own, they're non-finite. It's only when you add a particular type of auxiliary (called, incidentally, a finite element) that they become finite and thus, marked for tense.

Let's go back to the *Bleak House* passage to see if we can make this situation less... bleak.
1. Fog creeping into the cabooses of collier-brigs
2. fog lying out on the yards
3. and hovering in the rigging of great ships
4. fog drooping on the gunwales of barges and small boats

These are all non-finite clauses. None of the verbs are marked for tense. How can you know that? You can use a question-tag probe, you'll be happy to hear. When you try to affix a question tag to the end of each of these clauses, you'll find that there's more than one possibility.
1. Fog creeping into the cabooses of collier-brigs, *isn't it?* or *wasn't it?*

2. fog lying out on the yards, *isn't it?* or *wasn't it?*
3. and hovering in the rigging of great ships, *isn't it?* or *wasn't it?*
4. fog drooping on the gunwales of barges and small boats, *isn't it?* or *wasn't it?*

And when you go back to the clauses themselves, you'll see the reason for this ambiguity. There's no *is* or *was* in any of them.

The auxiliary in the question tag is always a finite element. If the finite element isn't in the clause, chances are you have a non-finite verb.

Creeping itself isn't marked for tense. It's only when we add the finite bit (the auxiliary) that we know whether we're in the present or the past. If the fog *is* creeping, we know it's creeping right now, today—present tense. If the fog *was* creeping, we know it was creeping sometime in the past, maybe earlier today, maybe yesterday, maybe 200 years ago—past tense.

But *creeping* (or any other -ing verb) on its own? It's out of time. It doesn't have a tense. It's non-finite.

Which is kind of perfect for the introductory chapter of a novel about the stagnancy of bureaucratic systems. Soon after this passage about fog, Dickens will explicitly link the members of the High Court of Chancery (the stagnant bureaucratic system his novel decries) as "mistily engaged in one of the ten thousand stages of an endless cause."[34]

Do you see what he did there? The cause is endless, the fog is endless, the *verbs* are endless—non-finite, without past, present or future.

What a great use of the grammatical palette!

A word on the grammatical palette

One of the joys of seeing grammar as a set of art supplies is that it enables you to "shape" or "colour" your writing to produce certain effects for the reader. Keep in mind that, like hues of paint, each grammatical feature can be used in an entirely creative way. You may wish to use non-finite clauses to depict a sense of timelessness, but timelessness can mean many things. In *Bleak House*, they contributed to an atmosphere of stagnancy. In other pieces they may do something entirely different.

In Theodore Roethke's poem, "Child on Top of a Greenhouse," for instance, the non-finite clauses produce the feeling of timelessness that we might remember from childhood.[35]

I once used non-finite clauses to play with the multiple meanings of the word *finite* in a piece of speculative flash fiction about a world in which language was a finite resource.[36]

There are so many ways to play!

Writing prompt: At a standstill

Think of a moment in your life when time seemed to stand still. Write a few sentences describing it.

Use the question-tag probe on each of your clauses to see whether they're finite or non-finite. If they're finite, make them non-finite. Usually you can do this just by removing the finite elements, or the auxiliaries. *Fog is creeping*, for instance, becomes *Fog creeping*. You may find that making this one change gives you ideas about other small shifts you could make to your writing.

Once you've made these changes, have a look at your piece again. Could you make it into a poem? Would it serve as the first paragraph to a story? Try it out with your friends or your writing group. Did the non-finite clauses create the effect you were going for?

Subject-verb agreement (or, why can't we all just get along?)

Now that you know how to discern whether a clause is finite or non-finite, you can confidently add non-finite verbs to your set of grammatical art supplies. But you may still be wondering about the criteria for finite verbs I mentioned above. A finite verb, I told you, is marked for tense and agrees with the subject.

What does it mean for a verb to agree with the subject?

You might not think you know what subject-verb agreement is, but (you'll be happy to know), your brain knows perfectly well.

To demonstrate this, indulge me with the following exercise. Fill in the blanks below with one of the following subject pronouns, *I, it* or *they*.

1. ___ is making a lot of noise
2. ___ am making a lot of noise
3. ___ are making a lot of noise

How easy was that exercise on a scale of 1-5? If English is one of your first languages, then I bet your answer was somewhere around 6. Would you like to know the answers? You don't need to know the answers! Your brain already knows.

Do keep in mind, though, that your brain might be

accessing a different variety of English from the brains of other English speakers. Different varieties have different structures—so please try to avoid grammar shaming yourself or others.

What's at the foundation of these structures? The *agreement* in subject-verb agreement has to do with grammatical terms known as *person* and *number*. There are three different types of person in English: *first person* (who's talking or speaking), *second person* (who's being addressed) and *third person* (who's being talked about). Keep in mind that person, especially third person, can refer to things as well as people. (I know, right?)

There are only two different types of number in English: singular (one) or plural (more than one or zero). Zero counts as plural. (I know, right?)

Remember when we said there were only seven subject pronouns in English? These are *I, he, she, it, we, you* and *they*. Each of these can be defined in terms of its grammatical person and number:

I: first person singular
He/she/it: third person singular
We: first person plural
You: second person plural
They: third person plural

And, as we've learned from our vast experience of using the question-tag probe, almost all the infinite combinations of words that can form the subject of a clause can be replaced with one of these seven subject pronouns. So if you're ever in doubt about whether a subject agrees with a verb in a given clause, just pull out your handy question-tag probe and test it out.

Imagine, for instance, that you've written the

following sentence. Your editor tells you the subject and verb don't agree.

The labyrinthian complexity of linguistic structures have been puzzling me all morning.

Is your editor right? You'll be thrilled to hear you can check by finding the subject and the finite using the question tag probe.

The labyrinthian complexity of linguistic structures have been puzzling me all morning, haven't **they**?

Now find the subject by finding what *they* refers to in your clause. It's pretty clear, right? *They* points to *linguistic structures.*

Or does it? Spoiler alert: the replacement test is going to reveal a snag.

The labyrinthian complexity of **they** *have been puzzling me all morning.*

You'll be right to think that sounds a little bizarre. That's because the subject element (the whole shebang) of your clause is actually *the labyrinthian complexity of linguistic structures.* The pronoun you would use to replace that phrase is *it.*

It *have been puzzling me all morning.*

The question-tag probe combined with the replacement test reveals that your editor—damn it all—is right, and the finite should be *has.*

The labyrinthian complexity of linguistic structures has been puzzling me all morning, hasn't it?

There's no need to worry about the labyrinthian complexity of linguistic structures. Your brain knows the way through.

If my brain knows the way through (I hear you ask), *then why do I keep getting subject-verb agreement wrong?*

Well, it's probably because you're writing dizzyingly complicated sentences, which can cause your brain to lose track for a minute. (Especially if it is thinking about cookies.) The good news is that you can always use the question-tag probe to get yourself (or your students) back on track.

Number and person remixed

Some of you may be raising a brow over your eagle eyes about the way I labelled the subject pronouns in terms of person and number:

I: first person singular
He/she/it: third person singular
We: first person plural
You: second person plural
They: third person plural

Can't *you* be used (I hear you ask) in the singular? Of course! So can *they*. But grammatically, *you* and *they* both agree with a plural finite, as you can see with the examples below (the finite is **underlined and in bold**).

*You **are** my friend, **are**n't you?*
*They **are** my friend, **are**n't they?*

In the second example, my friend is someone whose pronouns are they/them. In the first example, my friend is you (regardless of what your pronouns are, or how you feel about pronouns).

Are you still my friend? If so, come join me in Chapter 7, where we get to play with the other things that make a verb finite—tense and mood. And as your friend, I can tell you that it's not going to make you tense. Or moody.

Exercise: Finite and dandy

Use the question-tag probe to help you decide whether the following clauses are finite or non-finite. Rewrite the non-finite ones to make them finite and the finite ones to make them non-finite.
1. Just a poet, standing in front of a question-tag probe, wondering what it can do for me
2. Feeling pretty confident about subjects, still quite tense about verbs
3. Getting back into the creative zone will not be easy for me
4. Surely screaming for ice cream isn't necessary
5. Disappointed about kids who refuse to follow simple instructions about staying out of her writing sanctuary

7 TOO TENSE TO BE IN THE MOOD

Time present and time past

Read any introductory book on linguistics and you're likely to find some mention of the properties of human language that make it unique—different from, for instance, animal forms of communication.[37] One of these is a property called *displacement*, and it's pithily explained by George Yule in his book *The Study of Language* as follows.

> When your dog says GRRR, it means GRRR, *right now*, because dogs don't seem to be capable of communicating GRRR, *last night, over in the park*. It contrast, human language users are normally capable of producing messages equivalent to GRRR, *last night, over in the park*, and then going on to say *In fact, I'll be going back tomorrow for some more*.[38]

What I love about Yule's translation of Fido's utterance is that he's treating GRRR as if it were a clause. Fido seems to be communicating what Halliday calls a "quantum of information,"[39] where someone's doing something,

something's happening or something's being done to someone. Listen closely enough to Fido's *GRRR* and you'll hear a deep yearning for subjects and finite verbs.

You are a human, not a dog, and I'm encouraging you to celebrate that right now by filling in the gaps below with a *be* auxiliary (*am, is, are, was* or *were*). Choose the one your human brain thinks best.
   1. Fifi ___ howling in the park right now
   2. Fifi ___ howling in the park last night

Did you go for *is* in Clause 1 and *was* in Clause 2? Good human! Have a biscuit. (I'd go for chocolate, not gravy-flavoured, but you do you.)

The thing to notice with that exercise is not your superiority to our canine friends, but rather that your brain seems to know which form of the *be* auxiliary indicates present tense (right now) and which form indicates past tense (last night). Here's another thing worth noticing. In the verb element (*is howling* or *was howling*), it's only the first part, the *be* auxiliary, that's marked for tense (*is* or *was*). The rest of the verb element (*howling*) stays the same.

Only the first part of the verb element is marked for tense... Guess what that means?

That's right! It means you can use the question-tag probe to discover the tense of the finite verbs in your finite clauses. Isn't that the coolest? Let's give it a try with the Eudora Welty paragraph from Chapter 3. Look at the clauses below and pay attention to the auxiliaries in the question tags.
   1. She said nothing more, *did she?*
   2. and, backing against the door, pushed it closed with her hip, *didn't she?*
   3. Her anger passed like a remote flare of elation,

didn't it?
4. Neatly avoiding the table where the coffee bag stood, she began to walk around the room, *didn't she?*
5. as if a teasing indecision, an untouched mystery, led her by the hand, *didn't it?*

Did you notice any patterns? Of course you *did*. (Sorry.) Each of the above clauses produces a *did* auxiliary in the question tag. You may remember that forms of *do* (*do, does, did*) in a question-tag probe indicate that the clause is in the simple aspect. And now you've learned that the auxiliary in the question tag is marked for tense. In this case, it's past tense. The tense-aspect combination of all the above finite clauses is past simple.

You figured that out just by looking at the question tag. Consider the implications! Next time your editor tells you you've been inconsistent with tenses, you've got a great way of fixing the problem without having to spend all evening trawling through grammar websites.

For laughs, let's have a look at what the Welty passage would look like if she'd kept it in the simple aspect, but shifted the tense from past to present.

> *She says nothing more and, backing against the door, pushes it closed with her hip. Her anger passes like a remote flare of elation. Neatly avoiding the table where the coffee bag stands, she begins to walk around the room, as if a teasing indecision, an untouched mystery, leads her by the hand.*

Now have a look at the clauses in isolation and their associated question tags.
1. She says nothing more, *does she?*
2. and, backing against the door, pushes it closed

with her hip, *doesn't she?*
3. Her anger passes like a remote flare of elation, *doesn't it?*
4. Neatly avoiding the table where the coffee bag stands, she begins to walk around the room, *doesn't she?*[40]
5. as if a teasing indecision, an untouched mystery, leads her by the hand, *doesn't it?*

The *do* auxiliary changes from *did* to *does* in the question tag when the tense shifts to the present.

Here's why you don't need to get tense about tense. The auxiliary in the question tag will reveal the tense of the finite clause. And question tags, as we know, are easy peasy lemon squeezy.

One caveat before you start trying this new trick out on all your favourite clauses. Remember when I mentioned in Chapter 5 that there are two types of auxiliary, primary and modal? It's only the primary auxiliaries in the question tags that are marked for tense. The modal auxiliaries are marked for mood, which we'll play with in the next section.

How do you know if something is a primary or a modal auxiliary? There are so few of them you could just memorise them. Or better yet, just memorise the primaries. There are only three of those: *do, be* and *have* (and their forms).

(If you need any help memorising these three words, you're welcome to my favourite mnemonic aid, which is to sing "do, be, do, be, have" to the tune of Frank Sinatra's "Strangers in the Night." You're welcome.)

To recap: you can figure out the tense of a finite verb by looking at the tense of the primary auxiliary in the question tag.

How do you know what the tense of the primary auxiliary is?

Trust me, your brain knows. And what makes it even easier for your brain is that there are only two marked tenses in English, past and present. (In English, future is expressed with the modal auxiliaries *will* and *shall*.)

To check whether your brain *really* knows, have a look at the following list of all the forms of *do, be* and *have* that show up in question-tag probes and shout out whether it's past or present.

DO
do *(past or present?)*
does *(past or present?)*
did *(past or present?)*
BE
am *(past or present?)*
is *(past or present?)*
are *(past or present?)*
was *(past or present?)*
were *(past or present?)*
HAVE
have *(past or present?)*
has *(past or present?)*
had *(past or present?)*

Easy, right? But I'll give you the answers anyway:

DO: do, does (present)*; did* (past)
BE: am, are, is (present); *was* (past)
HAVE: have, has (present); *had* (past)

Would you like a poster version of this cheat sheet to hang in your classroom or office? I've made one available for you on my Refreshing Grammar resources page:

jodieclark.com/refreshingresources.

In my experience, the only time students get the past/present test wrong is when they're speeding through it so quickly they haven't stopped to consult their brains. If a student tells me that *were* is present tense, I have a quick way to get them back on track. "What would it be if it were past tense?" I ask. They usually realise straight away that it's already past tense.

Sometimes your brain needs to access the past to know the present, and vice versa. (Put that on a t-shirt.)

Writing prompt: Get present

Write five sentences describing what you did yesterday. (*I woke up, I went to work, I danced with reckless abandon in the photocopy room, I got caught, I died of humiliation.* For instance.)

Use the question-tag probe to find out what tense your finite verbs are in. (*I woke up*, didn't I? *Did* = past.)

Rewrite each clause, changing the finite verb so it's in the other tense. (If it's in the past tense, change it to the present and vice versa.)

Try also rewriting the clauses so that they produce different auxiliaries in the question tags. (Mine might be *I have woken up* or *I was waking up*.) What this does is change the *aspect* of your finite verb. *Have* auxiliaries often indicate *perfect* aspect and *be* auxiliaries often indicate *progressive* aspect.

Does changing the tense and aspect of the verbs in your description create different impressions when you read them back? Can you say what the different qualities of the rewrites are?

Feeling moody?

I'm guessing you're actually in a pretty good mood by now, given everything that the question-tag probe can do for you when it comes to verbs. And if not, I'm sure a few bars of that catchy Sinatra number (*Do, be, do, be, have…*) will perk you right up.

I regret to inform you that I don't have an earworm mnemonic for the modal auxiliaries, so I'll just list them again here for you to bookmark: *can, could, shall, should, will, would, may, might* and *must*.

To recap: when a primary auxiliary shows up in your question-tag probe, you know the clause is marked for tense. When a modal auxiliary shows up, you know the clause is marked for mood. What's the difference?

When we're situating something in time (tense), we're acting as if the thing we're talking or writing about is certain. When we're using modals, we're invoking what M. A. K. Halliday calls a "a region of uncertainty,"[41] which feels to me like something that should be written on 16th century maps next to "Here be dragons."

You can tell the difference with the following two sentences.
 1. I won the lottery.
 2. I would buy you a drink if I won the lottery.

Two quick question tags will let you know whether we're in the region of certainty or uncertainty.
 1. I won the lottery, **didn't I**?
 2. I would buy you a drink if I won the lottery, **wouldn't I**?[42]

The question tag for sentence 1, *did*, is the past tense

form of the primary auxiliary, *do*, so we know we're in the region of certainty. The main finite clause in sentence 2 has a verb with a modal auxiliary, *would*, which puts us in the realm of uncertainty. This is probably a good thing. Feeling overly certain about a lottery win is rarely a good reason to max out the credit card, especially on overpriced gin-based cocktails.

Get realis

These linguistically marked regions of certainty and uncertainty are also known as *realis mood* and *irrealis mood*, respectively. And you'll be happy to know we don't need expensive alcoholic beverages to have fun with these.

Writing prompt: Misty water-coloured memories

Write about a time when you were embarrassed, humiliated or mortified as a child. Separate out the finite clauses of your narrative and affix a question tag to each. Do the auxiliaries in the tags indicate your clauses are in realis or irrealis mood? (As a reminder, primary auxiliaries (*do, be, have*) indicate realis and modal auxiliaries (*can, could, shall, should, will, would, may, might and must*) indicate irrealis.)

How realis did you get with this exercise? Did you dredge up something *really* embarrassing?

Maya Angelou certainly did in the opening scene of *I Know Why the Caged Bird Sings*. If there's anything more mortifying than wetting yourself in church, I'm not sure what it is. Here's Angelou's extraordinarily well crafted scene.

> The giggles hung in the air like melting clouds that were waiting to rain on me. I held up two fingers, close to my chest, which meant that I had to go to the toilet, and tiptoed toward the rear of the church. Dimly, somewhere over my head, I heard ladies saying, "Lord bless the child," and "Praise God." My head was up and my eyes were open, but I didn't see anything. Halfway down the aisle, the church exploded with "Were you there when they crucified my Lord?" and I tripped over a foot stuck out from the children's pew. I stumbled and started to say something, or maybe to scream, but a green persimmon, or it could have been a lemon, caught me between the legs and squeezed. I tasted the sour on my tongue and felt it in the back of my mouth.[43]

A quick look at the first clauses in this passage reveal that Angelou has situated the scene firmly in the past, in the realis mood.

1. The giggles hung in the air... **didn't they?**
2. I held up two fingers... **didn't I?**
3. I tiptoed... **didn't I?**
4. ...I heard ladies saying... **didn't I?**
5. My head was up, **wasn't it?**
6. and my eyes were open, **weren't they?**
7. but I didn't see anything, **did I?**

My own descriptions of memories from my past are usually situated, like Angelou's, in the past tense, firmly in the realis. Does that make me a creative writing genius?

Unfortunately, no. In a study of *Caged Bird*, Sana Imtiaz Choudhry and Saiqa Imtiaz Asif argue that Angelou's genius lies in her ability to draw upon her everyday embodied experiences to shed light on wider cultural issues, such as race, class and gender oppression.[44] Our explorations into realis and irrealis can help us appreciate how Angelou frames the scene that depicts her embarrassing moment in church.

Let's return to the description of the young child, standing in front of the congregation, struggling to remember the poem she's supposed to be reciting. Angelou depicts her child self as looking out at the churchgoers and imagining what they're thinking about her. In her description of this imagining, Angelou artfully uses the irrealis mode to pull us into the region of uncertainty, which reveals the young girl's desires.

> *Wouldn't they be surprised when one day I woke out of my black ugly dream, and my real hair, which was long and blond, would take the place of the kinky mass that Momma wouldn't let me straighten?... Then they would understand why I had never picked up a Southern accent, or spoke the common slang, and why I had to be forced to eat pigs' tails and snouts.*[45]

Using the question-tag probe on these clauses shows us a host of modal auxiliaries cropping up. (We don't need a tag for clause 1 because it's already in the form of a question.)

1. ***Wouldn't they*** be surprised when one day...
2. my real hair, which was long and blond, would take the place of the kinky mass... ***wouldn't it?***
3. Then they would understand why I had never picked up a Southern accent, ***wouldn't they?***

The introductory scenes of Angelou's memoir offer invaluable insights about socially impactful life writing. The description of the awkward, frightened girl embarrassing herself in church is relatable to almost anyone who's ever been a child in an adult world. We can all tell stories about childhood mortification, and chances are we'd use the realis mode to do so.

　Not everyone can tell stories, though, about longing to be White. White people, especially, can't tell these stories. Angelou crafts this longing through the imagery, voice and, significantly, the *grammar* of the clauses in her passage. Her use of modal auxiliaries reveals some of the ways that race-based hierarchies inscribe themselves into the minds and bodies of Black children.

Writing prompt: Transforming memories

> Go back to the embarrassing moment you wrote about earlier. Did you feel connected to your child self when you wrote it? If so, bring yourself back into your adult consciousness, with all you know about structural inequality and oppression. Can you write some of that awareness into your original piece without losing the child's perspective? You might find it helpful to play with irrealis mode here. Write some clauses using modal auxiliaries (*can, could, shall, should, will, would, may, might* and *must*). What do these modals allow you to express?

You can have *all* the cookies now

If making it to the end of the seventh chapter of a grammar textbook isn't a reason to reward yourself, I don't know what is. It's not just that you've ploughed through all the content. It's also the immense amount you've learned in doing so. By now I bet you feel confident about finding the subject and verb elements of clauses, spotting the difference between finite and non-finite verbs and identifying the tense or mood of a finite clause. More importantly, you've found ways of experimenting with all this new grammatical knowledge and of allowing it to inspire you as you create your masterpieces. And hopefully you've had fun in the process.

You are very welcome to stop here if you'd like.

I'll be honest. In the work I do with grammatical structures (and by work, I should say *play*), I don't tend to need more than the subject and verb of a clause. This is true of my analytic and my creative work.

But wait, I hear you say. What about the other clause elements? Didn't you mention complements and adjuncts? And you promised to explain why you use complement *rather than* object. *And also, can't you please say something, even just a little bit, about word class?*

Overachievers, I hear you. The next chapters are for you.

Exercise: All tensed up and nowhere to go

Use the question-tag probe to find the subject and verb elements of each of the following clauses. Use the auxiliary in the question tag to determine whether it's in the past or present tense. Then rewrite the clause so it's in the other tense.

1. George's dog has been saying *GRRR* quite a lot recently
2. Fido clearly had things to talk about
3. I have never heard the song "Strangers in the Night"
4. That's making it difficult to remember the primary auxiliaries
5. I wanted a catchy tune for the modals, too

8 WITH MY COMPLEMENTS (FOR THE OVERACHIEVERS)

It's fun to play with the SVCA

Remember when we were talking about Elli's remarkable ability, at the green age of two years and eight months, to produce a clause with all the possible clause elements, in the order most likely to be found in English? She did it once with *Jake take my blocks away* and again with *Elli give it back by myself.* Talk about an overachiever!

The four possible clause elements are subject (S), verb (V), complement (C) and adjunct (A), and we can say we're doing an "SVCA analysis" when we locate them.[46]

Here's the SVCA analysis for the first clause.

Subject (S): Jake
Verb (V): take
Complement (C): my blocks
Adjunct (A): away

And here it is for the second.

S: *Elli*
V: *give*
C: *it*
A: *back*
A: *by myself*

Finite clauses will have only one subject element and one verb element. Usually, they'll only have one complement, but there are occasions when you'll find two. Clauses can have an infinite number of adjuncts, as with the following clause that no one ever uttered.

Unfortunately, much to my great regret, the snivelling excuse for a sibling that my parents produced without my approval will have by now embezzled those few humble tokens that I dare call my own without the smallest hint of remorse, without even a whiff of compunction, without concern for anything but his own selfish gain...

Here's the SVCA analysis of that one:

S: *The snivelling excuse for a sibling that my parents produced without my approval*
V: *will have embezzled*
C: *those few humble tokens that I dare call my own*
A: *Unfortunately*
A: *much to my great regret*
A: *by now*
A: *without the smallest hint of remorse*
A: *without even a whiff of compunction*
A: *without concern for anything but his own selfish gain*
(ad[junct] infinitum)

Are you starting to stress because you didn't spot all those adjuncts? Stress not! I haven't even told you what an adjunct is yet. Also, the beauty of SVCA analysis is that you don't even really need to know what each element is, just how to find it. And we can use probes to find the C and the A with (almost) as much success as the question-tag probe helps us find the S and the V.

The secret to using the probes is that, once you've committed to doing an SVCA analysis, you have to find each element *in order*. In other words, don't try to find the A until you've eliminated the S and the V, and then found the C (if there is one).

If you're having trouble remembering to go in order, feel free to use my mnemonic, which is to sing "SVCA" to the tune of "YMCA" by the Village People (dance moves optional).

You're welcome.

I'm giving you a new probe. I'm giving *who, what?*

If you're as in love with the question-tag probe as I am, then it might be a bit troubling to learn that once we've found the S and the V, the question tag loses its usefulness. Finding the C (the complement) requires a new probe.

To ease the transition from one probe to another, I'm going to show you the transcript of my conversation with Elli again, which has a beautiful example of how question tags show up interpersonally in the wild.

> Elli: Jake take my blocks away!
> Jodie: Did he? Here.

What makes it possible for me to respond with a question tag ("Did he?") is that Elli's utterance is a finite clause. One other thing to notice is that the auxiliary in my question tag—*did*—shows that I'm treating Elli's verb *take* as if it were in the past tense. I'm unconsciously "other correcting" her *take* to *did take*, or *took*.

Now imagine if Elli only produced the first part of her utterance and said, "Jake take." Her utterance has an S and a V, so it seems to fulfil the minimum criteria for being a clause.

But I think the three-year-old in my brain would feel like something was missing.

And perhaps my response to "Jake take" would not have been "Did he?" but rather "Jake took *what*?"

The brains of most three-year-olds know that there are some verbs in the English language that don't do well on their own. *Take* is one of them. It's called a *transitive verb*, which means that it requires an object, or a noun phrase that answers the question *who?* Or *what?* after the subject and the verb.

S: *Jake*
V: *take*
O: *my blocks*

We could replace the noun phrase *my blocks* with any number of other noun phrases that Jake might have taken from Elli: *my blocks, my book, my faith in brotherly love*. All these answer the question "Jake took *what*?" If the noun phrases that describe what Jake has taken refer to humans *(my best friend, my teacher, Santa Claus)*, then the question becomes "Jake has taken *who*?"[47]

And thus we have a new probe, a probe to find the complement. Find your S, find your V and then ask S...V... *who* or *what*?

The answer to *who* or *what*? is (almost always) the complement (C).

Let's try it with a few of our earlier examples.
1. But I covered Ollie's shift yesterday
2. She said nothing more
3. as if a teasing indecision, an untouched mystery, led her by the hand
4. Like you've just been handed a great big wad of Time

We know better than to start finding complements before finding subjects and verbs, so first we'll use our question-tag probe to remind ourselves of the subjects and verbs of the above clauses.
1. But (S I) (V covered) Ollie's shift yesterday, *didn't I?*
2. (S She) (V said) nothing more, *did she?*
3. as if (S a teasing indecision, an untouched mystery,) (V led) her by the hand, *didn't it?*
4. Like (S you) (V… 've) just (…V been handed) a great big wad of Time, *haven't you?*

Now your job is simple. Just say S…V…*who* or *what?*
1. (S I) (V covered) *what?*
2. (S She) (V said) *what?*
3. (S a teasing indecision, an untouched mystery,) (V led) *who?*
4. (S you) (V 've been handed) *what?*

The answer to *who* or *what* is (most of the time) the complement.
1. (S I) (V covered) (C Ollie's shift)
2. (S She) (V said) (C nothing more)
3. (S a teasing indecision, an untouched mystery,) (V led) (C her)
4. (S you) (V 've been handed) (C a great big wad of Time)

It's possible for a clause to have two complements. If

you've ever heard of direct and indirect objects or object complements you'll know what I'm talking about. If you haven't heard (or don't want to hear) of these, don't worry. Just remember that sometimes after asking *who* or *what?* after the SV you'll find yourself asking *who* or *what?* again. Here are some examples:

1. (S Someone) (V has handed) (C you) (C a great big wad of Time)
2. (S Elli's brother) (V is giving) (C her) (C a headache)
3. (S That teasing indecision, that untouched mystery) (V is driving) (C me) (C crazy)

Now's probably a good time to admit that I don't love the *who/what* probe as much as I love the question-tag probe. I want to marry the question-tag probe. The *who/what* probe and I are just good friends. I've found in the classroom that it's less failsafe. One problem is that if students haven't accurately identified the S and the V, then asking *who* or *what* will lead them astray.

Imagine, for instance, in clause 2, where the student decides (accurately) that *Elli's brother* is the subject and then decides (inaccurately) that *is* is the verb element. Then when they ask *Elli's brother is what?* they get the answer *giving her a headache*, which sounds OK, but it's not the complement. One problem here is that *who* and *what* are commonly used when we're asking someone to repeat a string of words, and this string of words doesn't always correspond to a clause element.

That said, there's an advantage to this aspect of the *who/what* probe that can actually help us, which is why it's still my friend. Have a look at the following clauses, which we've seen before. Go ahead and use the question-tag probe to find the subject and verb elements.

1. The pleasure of making a daisy-chain would be worth the trouble of getting up and picking the daisies
2. Once upon a time he had been a track cyclist

Is this what you got?

1. (S The pleasure of making a daisy-chain) (V would be) worth the trouble of getting up and picking the daisies, *wouldn't it?*
2. Once upon a time (S he) (V had been) a track cyclist, *hadn't he?*

Now let's try the same thing we did with Elli's clauses. Let's reduce them to just their subjects and verbs and see if they still work as finite clauses.

1. The pleasure of making a daisy chain would be
2. He had been

Is your red-pen hand just aching to circle these and label them incomplete sentences? But they have subjects and finite verbs, which is the minimum that finite clauses are supposed to have, right?

We've now learned that transitive verbs also require objects, or noun phrases that answer the question *who?* or *what?* Since the above clauses need an answer to *who?* or *what?* we might be tempted to think they have transitive verbs.

As it happens, the verbs in clause 1 (*would be*) and 2 (*had been*) are *not* transitive verbs. They're copular verbs. According to traditional grammatical analysis, copular verbs don't take *objects*, they take *complements*. Complements can be noun phrases or adjective phrases.[48]

The good news for us is that *complement* is an umbrella term that encompasses both the objects of transitive verbs and the complements of copular verbs. So we don't need to spend a lot of time worrying whether a verb is

transitive, intransitive, copular, inopular or popular. Just kidding. There's no such thing as an inopular verb. I guess there might be such a thing as a popular verb, but it's not a technical term. The key takeaway here is that *complement* is a one-stop shop as the clause element that (most of the time) responds to the *who/what* probe.
Check it out:
1. (S The pleasure of making a daisy chain) (V would be) *what?*
2. (S He) (V had been) *what?*

The answer to *what?* in clause 1 is the adjective phrase *worth the trouble of getting up and picking the daisies* and in 2 it's the noun phrase *a track cyclist*.

Writing prompt: Transitivity in steamy scenes

If all this talk of copular verbs is making you want to write the next scene in your romance novel or lyrics for a racy love song, then this prompt is for you. Think of as many transitive verbs as you can that have to do with gettin' up close and personal with your special someone(s). I thought of *kissed, hugged* and *squeezed*, but no judgments from me if yours are a bit less G-rated.

Now choose your favourite subjects and complements for these verbs. Start with single words, maybe pronouns. *I kissed him. She kissed me. They kissed him.* Etc. Have some flirty pronoun fun.

Now expand your subjects and complements so that they're more than one word. At first this may involve kissing body parts, as in *I kissed that cute little dent above his right eyebrow.* But you might find yourself getting even more flexible about what types of subjects can kiss what types of complements. *An ancient longing deep within me kissed those overflowing eyes* or *I kissed the space between us.*

Some verbs just can't take a complement

All finite clauses have subject and verb elements, but they don't always have a complement. We've spoken about transitive and copular verbs, which seem to beg the *who/what* probe when you use them on their own. For instance: *You took* what? *You picked* what? *You feel* what? *You heard* what?

Now try the following clause and see what the *who/what* probe does:

Pigs fly gracefully.

Does it work to ask *Pigs fly what?*

Well, yes and no. It kind of works, if by *what?* you mean *Heh? I didn't quite catch the thing you said after "fly."*

If you ask it that way, the response would be *gracefully*, which isn't a complement.

But the slightly tricky thing about the *who/what* probe is that it doesn't work if you're seeing it as a way of getting people to repeat themselves. The secret instead is to ask yourself whether *who?* or *what?* are the right questions.

For *Pigs fly gracefully*, a better question would be *Pigs fly how?*

How? isn't a probe for finding the complement. So with *Pigs fly gracefully*, there's no complement. *Fly*, in this clause, is an intransitive verb.

You *could* make a list of all the intransitive verbs to save yourself the trouble of wasting your precious probes on them. But I wouldn't recommend it. Many verbs can be either transitive or intransitive depending on how they're used. Take *fly*, for instance. What would make *fly* a transitive verb? What phrase could go in the complement slot of the following?

(S Pigs) (V fly) (C _____)

Doing this exercise with students is fun because it's hard for them to get the answer when they're picturing winged pigs gracing the blue skies. I make it even harder by projecting that exact image onto the screen at the front of the room. This is a teaching practice known as "setting your students up for failure so that you feel smug when they can't get the answer."

Here are the answers they give when they're looking at the winged pigs. *In the sky?* Not a complement. *Every day?* Not a complement. *With difficulty?* Nope! (Snigger, snigger, snigger.)

If you've found some examples of "right" answers, I hope you're feeling smug.

(S Pigs) (V fly) (C airplanes)
(S Pigs) (V fly) (C kites)
(S Pigs) (V fly) (C flags)

Hopefully it's clear that the complements *airplanes, kites* and *flags* answer the *what?* question, whereas the other possibilities answer other questions, like *where? when?* or *how?* If you find yourself giving a *where, when* or *how* answer to a *who/what* probe, you've probably not landed on a complement.

What's possibly more interesting for me about the "Pigs fly" exercise is the different qualities of the same verb when it's transitive or intransitive. The subject of the intransitive verb *fly* (whether it's a pig or some other adventurous creature) is someone or something that is moving through the air on its own. Someone who's flying something else (transitive) can do so with their feet firmly on the ground (as is the case with *flying kites* or *flying flags*). Or, if they're flying airplanes, they're completely dependent on the machine to keep them in the air.

When I think about this too much, it makes my brain buzz a little.

In a good way.

But what about all the "wrong" answers—*gracefully, in the sky, every day, with difficulty?*

We'll discuss these in the next chapter. Hopefully, without difficulty.

Exercise: "You're worth the whole damn bunch put together"

You may recognise the above quote as the only compliment Nick Carraway ever gave Gatsby.[49] Fortunately for us, the first several clauses of *The Great Gatsby* offer us quite a few complements. I've listed some of them below, with minor adjustments to suit this exercise.

I've labelled the subjects and verbs for you. Your job is simply to decide if the remaining bracketed elements are complements.

Remember: if they're complements, they'll answer the question SV *what?* or SV *who?* and you can safely label them with a C. If the bracketed element answers a different question, it's likely not a complement. Some of the clauses have two complements, some have one and some have none.

Top tip: the elements below that aren't complements are adjuncts. If you want to be an overachiever you can give them an A.

(You already get an A, regardless of how well you do on this exercise.)

1. (S My father) (V gave) (? me) (? some advice)
2. (S I) (V 've been turning) (? it) (? over) (? in my mind) (? ever since)
3. (S All the people in this world) (V haven't had) (? your advantages)
4. (S The white palaces of fashionable East Egg) (V glittered) (? along the water) (? across the courtesy bay)
5. (S The history of the summer) (V begins) (? on that evening).

9 ADDING JUNK WITH ADJUNCTS

A linguist saves the world

When I heard that Ted Chiang's science fiction novella, *The Story of Your Life* had been made into a film, I rushed out to see it. The protagonist is a linguist, and understanding the structure of human language is a key plot point. In the film it's even better, because the linguist (spoiler alert) saves the world. Plus, it has aliens. I'm a big fan of aliens.[50]

A linguist saves the world! Out of all the professions of protagonists who victoriously battle the catastrophic event in apocalyptic disaster plots, linguist doesn't rank high. Superhero, yes. NASA scientist, yes. Paleoclimatologist? I'm looking at you, *The Day After Tomorrow*. *Ghostbusters* features Columbia University professors. Drillers get the laurels in *Armageddon*. But a linguist?

Writing prompt: The least likely hero

Sketch out an apocalyptic disaster plot with a world-saving hero. Choose a profession for your protagonist that no one would ever expect. Imagine ways to make underrated aspects of that profession pivotal to the mission. Maybe your hero is a pet groomer whose ability to clip toenails on frightened chihuahuas is just what's needed to detonate a bomb attached to an aggravated alien scorpion.

I loved both the film *Arrival* and the novella *The Story of Your Life*, and not just because they made me feel like being a linguist was supercool. They illustrate some of the ways that language shapes our human experience, and speculate on how non-human languages might produce different types of knowledge and ways of being.

Specifically, they focused on how human language shapes our experience of time.

The advantage of the novella is that this theme is woven into the grammatical structure of the clauses that comprise the story. Have a look at the first three finite clauses.[51]

    1. Your father is about to ask me the question
    2. This is the most important moment in our lives
    3. I want to pay attention, note every detail

Have you already stuck question tags at the end of these (*isn't he?* for 1, *isn't it?* for 2 and *don't I?* for 3)? Have you already spotted the subject, verb and complement? If so, I'm impressed. It may not be the most important moment in your life, but I'd count it up there in the top 100. Here's what I get.

    1. (S Your father) (V is) (C about to ask me the question)
    2. (S This) (V is) (C the most important moment in our lives)
    3. (S I) (V want) (C to pay attention, note every

detail)

There are so many things to note about the structure of these clauses, but for now it's worth just focusing on the tense of each of them. The auxiliaries in the question tags —*is, is* and *do*—indicate straight away that we're in the present tense.

It's not unusual for writers and speakers to use the present tense to narrate events that occurred in the past. This strategy is known as the historical present, or the conversational historical present when it's used in a spoken exchange.

It's clear from the last sentence of the first paragraph of *The Story of Your Life* that, despite the use of present tense, the narrative events are firmly rooted in the past. The question the narrator is about to be asked is "Do you want to make a baby?" It's also clear that the baby they're about to make is the "you" to whom the narrator is addressing her story. "I'd love to tell you the story of this evening," she continues, "the night you're conceived, but the right time to do that would be when you're ready to have children of your own, and we'll never get that chance."[52]

With these first sentences, the reader is drawn into a story of a whole life, with a hint of a tragic outcome, which begins at the moment when the couple decide to have a child. It's told in the present tense, but it feels like Mom is looking back on that life-changing moment and starting her story there.

By the time we get to the end, we'll realise our mistake. The story is not told in the historical present, but in the *actual* present. In acquiring the alien language (called "Heptapod B"), the protagonist has also acquired a nonlinear perception of time, so she knows what's going to happen in her life before it occurs. Have a look at the third paragraph from the end to see how Chiang achieves this grammatically.

> *Working with the heptapods changed my life. I met your father and learned Heptapod B, both of which make it possible for me to know you now, here on the patio in the moonlight. Eventually, many years from now, I'll be without your father, and without you. All I will have left from this moment is the heptapod language. So I pay close attention, and note every detail.*[53]

I know you're busy putting question tags at the end of all the clauses, but there are some tricky ones in there, so I'll do it for you (and take the rap if any of them are wrong).

1. (S Working with the heptapods) (V changed) (C my life) *[didn't it?]*
2. (S I) (V met) (C your father) *[didn't I?]*
3. and (S I) (V learned) (C Heptapod B) *[didn't I?]*
4. (S both of which) (V make) (C it) (C possible...) *[don't they?]*
5. ...for (S me) (V to know) (C you) (A now,) (A here) (A on the patio) (A in the moonlight) *[non-finite clause]*

We can tell from the auxiliaries in the question tags of the finite clauses (*did, did, did* and *do*) that the tense shifts from past (in clauses 1-3) to present (in clause 4). I can imagine a grammatically keen but unobservant proofreader tracing a blithe circle around the verb *make* in clause 4, and telling Chiang to change it to *made*.

But the final, non-finite clause tells us no mistake has been made. The three adjuncts in this clause position us in space (*here, on the patio, in the moonlight*) and time (*now*). These, not coincidentally, are the same space and time as the introductory paragraph. The whole story is told *now, here, on the patio, in the moonlight*. These adjuncts link the beginning to the end and initiate us into a world where there is no beginning or end, where it all exists at once.

Pretty powerful things, adjuncts, aren't they? So what's all this talk of "adding junk?"

Now, here, on the patio, in the moonlight

Remember when I said that SVCA analysis needs to be done in order? Use the pronoun in the question-tag probe to find the S, use the auxiliary in the probe to find the V, use the *who/what* probe to find the C (if there is one) or both the Cs (if there are two). Don't look for adjuncts (A) until you're certain about all the others.

I advise this because I don't have a reliable probe for adjuncts. The best I can tell you is that they're grammatically optional. They don't need to be there for a clause to feel well formed. Also, they can sneak their way into almost any position in the clause—at the beginning, in the middle, at the end, even in the middle of verb elements. So, if it's a helpful mnemonic, you can think of adjuncts as "added junk."

Now might be a good time for a set of steps in doing SVCA analysis.

Subject (S)
Find it by using the question-tag probe. What does the pronoun in the tag point to? For example: **Aisha** has lost her watch, *hasn't **she***?
Verb (V)
Find the finite part of the verb by using the question-tag probe. What does the auxiliary point to? For example:

Aisha **has lost** her watch, **_has_**_n't she?_
Complement (C)
Find it by asking _who?_ or _what?_ after the SV. For example: Aisha has lost _what?_ **her watch**.
Adjunct (A)
These are usually grammatically optional. Find it by looking at what's left over after your SVC analysis. What elements could be left out? What elements could change position in the clause? For example: Aisha has lost her watch **again**. **Again**, Aisha has lost her watch. Aisha has **again** lost her watch.

(Would you like a poster version of this cheat sheet to hang in your classroom or office? I've made one available for you my Refreshing Grammar resources page: jodieclark.com/refreshingresources.)

Let's try the whole process with a clause from _I Know Why the Caged Bird Sings_.

one day I woke out of my black ugly dream[54]

Hopefully by now you're singing the catchy SVCA theme song (dance moves optional). You've started finding the subject by sticking a question tag at the end.

one day (S I) woke out of my black ugly dream, didn't **I**?

And you've probably already found the verb, using the auxiliary in the question tag.

one day (S I) (V woke) out of my black ugly dream, **did**n't I?

And now you're stringing S and V together and asking _who_ or _what?_

I woke who? *I woke* what?

And you realise there's no answer to either of these

questions. There *might* have been an answer, of course. If the clause was *I woke my brother* or *I woke my dog* or even *I woke myself*, we'd have an answer to *who* or *what?* and that answer (*my brother, my dog, myself*) would be the complement. But *woke* is a verb that can be transitive or intransitive, and here it's intransitive, which means it doesn't need a complement.

So now we're onto the adjuncts. These, we know, are the elements that could be left out. Seems easy enough, right? It is, with one caveat. Don't get out your editor's red pen and look for individual words that could be left out, like *black* and *ugly*. You need to look for entire constituents, complete elements, the whole shebang.

The way to test this is to see which elements could move to another place in the clause. (This doesn't always work, but it works with enough consistency to give it a try.) Let's test it with *one day*. Can we move it to the end?

(S I) (V woke) out of my black ugly dream (one day)

Yes, we can! So *one day* is an adjunct.

(A one day) (S I) (V woke) out of my black ugly dream

How about *out of my black ugly dream?*

(A one day) (out of my black ugly dream) (S I) (V woke)

It works! It's an adjunct. We could play around even more with these adjuncts and create a whole set of differently shaped clauses.

> one day I woke out of my black ugly dream
> out of my black ugly dream one day I woke
> one day I, out of my black ugly dream, woke

So we can say with some confidence that the SVCA analysis is

(A one day) (S I) (V woke) (A out of my black ugly dream)

Writing prompt: I'm dreaming of a moveable adjunct

Write a poem where the subject and verb of each clause is *I dream*. With each line, add an adjunct, or move around the adjuncts you've already written. For instance: *(S I) (V dream) (A of kittens). (S I) (V dream) (A of kittens) (A in the sunlight). (A Now) (S I) (S dream) (A of kittens) (A by starlight). (A Unfortunately,) (S I) (V dream) (A of kittens) (A endlessly).* Note: your version won't have the labels and the brackets, unless you want your poem to have a metalinguistic flavour, in which case you won't hear any complaints from me.

Guess what? You now know everything you need to know about clauses to analyse the elements of all the finite clauses you meet in the wild. (With a bit of jiggery pokery you'll find you can analyse the elements of non-finite clauses too.) Hopefully you're feeling a lot more confident about grammar than you felt when you started. Even more hopefully you're brimming with ideas about how to use these grammatical principles to inspire your writing and your teaching. You're reciting question tags in your sleep. And maybe you're dreaming about adjuncts.

Before you rush off, and while we're on the topic of dreaming, may I share one more way in which grammar fascinates and delights me?

Exercise: Who you callin' junk?

Do an SVCA analysis of the following clauses. When you're done, have a cookie. And then have a good look at the adjuncts.

Adjuncts, as we know, are not junk. That said, you could remove them without affecting the sentence too much grammatically. They also can be moved to other places in the clause.

Once you've done the SVCA analysis and enjoyed your cookie, rewrite each clause, experimenting with all the places the adjunct or adjuncts could go.

1. All films should contain world-saving linguists, in my opinion
2. A plumber would be a good choice as the hero of an apocalyptic disaster plot
3. Alien languages really would be fun to learn
4. Grammatical analysis has actually become my favourite way to spend an afternoon
5. I would never have believed it before

10 GRAMMAR FOR DREAMERS

What are your dreams?

You may remember that at the beginning of this book I told you I didn't think you needed a book on grammar. And yet, here you are, reading the final chapter! I'm thrilled you made it this far. While you're here, can I ask a question?

Has this book fulfilled your grammar dreams?

What an absurd thing to ask. People don't have grammar dreams, do they?

I once had a *Sex in the City* dream where one of the characters confessed to having an affair with a vicar and I discovered the etymology of the word *vicarious*, but that's more semantics than syntax and... Wait. Am I oversharing?

So if you're not dreaming about grammar, what are you dreaming about? Or if your life has become too mired in everyday reality for dreams, what did you once dream about? What were your dreams from childhood and young adulthood?

My biggest dream was to be a writer. At the age of seven, when people asked me what I wanted to be when I grew up, the response was invariable. "A famous author," I'd say with blithe assurance.

Some context might help to attenuate the seeming arrogance of that ambition. I'd just finished the first novel I ever read, *Superfudge* by Judy Blume, and it blew my mind. Blume, a grown woman, had written the story as if she were an eleven-year-old boy. It was my first lesson in first-person point of view, and it stuck with me.

My dad, noticing how enraptured I was by this literary experience, asked what I was reading. I managed to show him the cover of my library book without removing my eyes from the page.

"Judy Blume," he said. "She's a famous author."

If he said anything else, I didn't catch it. *A famous author*, I thought. *That's what I want to be.*

And I more or less continued dreaming about being *a famous author* (I eventually changed my response to "fiction writer") until my early twenties. At that point I enrolled in a master's degree in linguistics at the University of Strasbourg. For my dissertation I analysed the use of the word *like* in everyday conversation. I discovered that *like* was used throughout my data to draw a line around whatever stretch of words follows it. I wrote in my dissertation that *like* draws a line around parts of the conversation, to single out particular thoughts and images as distinct.

With this discovery my love affair with linguistics began.

I loved linguistics so much, I... Well, I didn't marry it, but I may as well have. I moved to the UK to do a PhD in it. It was at that point that I discovered Critical Discourse Analysis (or CDA), which is a method of analysing language to uncover oppressive social structures.

I wasn't new to social injustice before that point, but I hadn't figured out what I was supposed to do about it. Studying CDA made me realise what every inspired activist already knows. Change comes about when passionate people direct their passions toward what needs to be transformed. I was in my early thirties, and I'd stumbled upon a new dream. To help create a more welcoming world.

The grammar of oppression

Fast forward about a decade. I'm sitting with one of my undergraduate students, Beth, in a university café after class. I pull out a notebook and draw a stick figure in the middle of the page.

"What I've noticed about you," I observe, "is how important it is to you to maintain your own integrity. You are steadfastly committed to being who you are, even when everyone around you is literally trying to beat that impulse out of you."

She stares wide-eyed at my drawing. "How can you see this?"

I'm so glad she asked. "It shows up in the grammatical patterns of your narrative about your group of friends."

Beth had agreed to be a participant in a study I conducted in 2013 called "Doing Identity Differently." I was collecting stories from people who'd experienced their identities being challenged in some way. Beth had been the victim of abuse and bullying when she was at school.

Analysing the transcript of her account of this experience blew my mind.

I started in the way I always start now, which is

to separate out the finite clauses of whatever text or conversation I'm studying. "When I started high school," Beth's story begins, "I got in with the wrong crowd." It takes her about 15 finite clauses to describe the abuse she suffered in the hands of that crowd.

All I needed to do was to find the subject and verb elements of these clauses (thank you, question-tag probe) to notice an interesting pattern.

Four of the clauses had *I* as a subject. The rest had *they*. *They* referred to "the wrong crowd."

I don't know how many people were actually part of Beth's crowd—maybe four, maybe fourteen—but grammatically speaking, there were only two participants. *I* and *they*. Beth versus the crowd.

Here's what the SVCA analysis looks like for the clauses in which Beth describes the crowd as being particularly abusive.

(S they) (V were putting) (C me) (A under boxes)

(S they) (V used to not let)[55] *(C me) (C get out)*

(S they) (V came and dumped)[56] *(C a load of water) (A on my hair)*
(S they) (V used to push) (C me) (A down)
(S they) (V used to try and hurt) (C me)
(S they) (V shoved) (C me) (A off a kerb)

The grammatical patterns here paint a picture of two participants: a they who's verbing a me. And all the lexical verbs have the same quality. Halliday calls them "transformative-contact"[57] processes, which depict actions in which someone or something changes someone or something by coming into physical contact with them.

At first glance it might seem like Beth is presenting

herself as the victim of the bullying actions of her peers. I see something else in it, though, something that I will share with Beth in our debriefing session after I've done a bit of analysis.

Beth originally describes herself as being *in* the wrong crowd.

If she really wanted to present herself as a part of that crowd, the subjects, verbs and complements in her clauses would not have been divided into *me (I)* and *them (they)*. Instead she would have spoken of *us (we)*—first person plural. The way she tells the story reveals that she wants to maintain the integrity of her individual, unique self, even in the face of pressure to conform.

What is required grammatically, I wondered, for her to keep that *me-them* division in place? What separates the *they* from the *me*?

The SVCA analysis shows it. When *they* is the subject and *me* is the complement, the thing that separates these is the verb. The transformative-contact verbs, where the bullies are doing harm to Beth's body. As I wrote in the book where I share this research, "the body serves as mediator between the norms of the crowd and the resistant self, enabling the integrity of the self ... to be preserved."[58]

I'm always fascinated by the insights that grammatical analysis can reveal, but the picture here is a depressing one. What kind of world is it where people are maintaining their sense of self by subjecting their bodies to abuse?

Fortunately, the bullying is only the first part of Beth's story. It's in the grammar of the second part that the real transformation occurs.

A more welcoming world

"When I was being bullied," Beth recounts, "one of my teachers noticed. He was the closest teacher I had."

He convinced her to join the school's drama club.

"The minute I joined drama," Beth reveals, "my world completely changed. I got into lasting friendships, with people who are still my friends now."

They put on a high-budget production of *We Will Rock You*.

"From that minute onwards," Beth says, "when I stepped off that stage, I knew I needed to keep with those friends I'd made, because they were so protective over me. They still are. I just knew that my life would never be the same again. Because the minute I started that, the bullying just stopped. It's like they saw me get confident and get a good group of friends around me and they just backed away."

Remember the story of me falling in love with linguistics? It began with the enlightening moment when I discovered how the word *like* was being used to draw a circle around whatever follows, to mark it as special.

When I looked closely at Beth's story, I realised that this encompassing quality is not limited to words like *like*.

All language does it.

And language doesn't just draw lines around thoughts and images, it also creates little envelopes of selfhood. I like to think of these as membranes, like cell membranes, which are selectively permeable. By letting some things in and keeping some things out, membranes make it possible for life (or ideas) to exist within the protective structures they form.

Have a look at my SVCA analysis of the last three clauses of Beth's account.

(S they) (V saw) (C me get confident)
(S they) (V saw) (C me get a good group of friends around me)

(S they) (A just) (V backed away)[59]

We still have *they* verbing *me* (Beth), but the quality of the verbs is different now. They're *seeing* her, not hurting her. What's protecting the integrity of Beth's selfhood is no longer the membrane of her body, but the membrane of her *new group of friends*.

I share this analysis with Beth later in the debrief, returning her attention to my stick figure drawing. "Look," I say. I draw a membrane around her. "You're protected." I draw other people, each with their own membranes. They surround her, enveloping her, holding her. Their membranes both protect their own individuality and reinforce hers.

"You are in a community that sees you for who you are," I tell her. "You are valued. You are safe."

Being seen, being valued, being safe. I felt like Beth—specifically, the grammar of Beth's courage in the face of adversity—has given me one of the secrets to creating a more welcoming world.[60]

You get to have more than one dream

Dreams, it turns out, are like clauses. They can be configured and reconfigured in an infinite number of ways. They are quanta of information about what could be transformed in the world, whether it's your own world or a bigger social world, or both.

I didn't have to drop my dream of being a fiction writer in order to pursue my love of linguistics and to create a more welcoming world. I get to do all of it.[61]

Some of your dreams may align with mine, some may be vastly different. Grammar, as it turns out, plays a role in all our dreams, because it's the way we structure our stories, in poetry, fiction and life. I hope this book has given you a new way of thinking about grammar. Maybe you have some ideas about how attention to grammatical structures can help create a more welcoming world.

Or at least, a more welcoming art room atmosphere.

Congratulations! You've achieved so much in just being willing to try out this refreshing approach to grammar.

Haven't you?

APPENDIX 1
WORD CLASS
FOR TEACHERS
WITH CLASS

Thank you so much for making it this far through the quest to create an art room atmosphere in a conversation about grammar. I'm hoping that this book has built your confidence in your own intuitive knowledge and given you some ideas about how grammatical structures can work like art supplies.

If you're a teacher, I'd be thrilled if you've already invited your students to have a go with the question-tag probe. I'm picturing your classroom, buzzing with students tagging their own and their neighbours' clauses, finding subjects and verb elements with reckless, joyful abandon. (A linguist can dream.)

And that's all well and good, your teacher self might be thinking. *But what about word class?* I hear you ask. *I have to teach word class. Is there an intuitive way to teach word class?*

Teachers, I see you. I honour your conscientiousness. And I'm happy to share with you how I teach word class, which I think is pretty intuitive (if I do say so myself). But the reason I'm including this information in an appendix and not in the main text is because I think clause elements are easier to grasp and better suited to creative writing and critical reading than word class. So if you don't have to teach word class, you are absolutely welcome to skip this appendix. No hard feelings. Go write your masterpiece!

Still with me? OK. Here's the other caveat. My approach to teaching word class works well if you use carefully designed, purpose-built examples. It's not great for clauses you find "in the wild," which tend to have a lot more interesting stuff going on. I don't mind using constructed examples with my own students because I think it helps them get a feel for what's nouny about nouns, what's adverby about adverbs, where prepositions are likely to show up, etc. Word class intuition takes a fair bit more time to build up than clause element intuition, which is usually pretty instantaneous once you've got the probes in place.

With all those provisos firmly in place, let's get to it.

Start with SVCA

I never ask my students to do word class spotting (find the nouns, find the verbs, etc.) because of all the frustration that creates. If I'm asking them to label the word classes in a clause, I encourage them to do an SVCA analysis first. If nothing else, it gives them extra SVCA practice, which can only be a good thing, right? And it also helps them situate words within the context of phrases and clause elements.

So let's start with a nice, clear-cut, well designed

example clause. We'll be labelling all the words in the clause, but we'll start with SVCA.

My horrible brother has thrown my favourite blocks in the bin again

By now I'm assuming this is second nature for you (and hopefully your students as well). You've found the question tag (*hasn't he?*), which has pointed you to the subject (*my horrible brother*) and the verb (*has thrown*). Then you asked *my horrible brother has thrown **what**?* And when you received the answer *my favourite blocks*, you knew to label that as the complement. You realised *in the bin* and *again* aren't grammatically necessary, and also that they could be moved around in the clause *Again, my horrible brother has thrown in the bin my favourite blocks!* So you recognised these to be adjuncts. Here's how it looks all nicely labelled.

(S My horrible brother) (V has thrown) (C my favourite blocks) (A in the bin) (A again)

Hopefully now you're smugly dunking a cookie in your steaming hot cup of tea.

Then identify the phrase type of each element

Now I'm going to let you know that the clause elements are very often (but by no means 100% of the time) realised by particular types of phrase.

Subjects are almost always realised by noun phrases.

Verb elements are always realised by verb phrases.

Complements are almost always realised by *either* adjective or noun phrases.

Adjuncts are almost always realised by *either* adverb or

prepositional phrases.

If you know that, and you're prepared that you'll meet some exceptions in the wild world of clauses,[62] then doing an SVCA analysis will get you one step closer to being able to label phrase types in a clause. If you've labelled your subject and verb correctly, you're on to a winner with at least one noun phrase and one verb phrase. Then when you get to complements and adjuncts, you know you've got a fifty-fifty chance with each.

So have another quick look at our SVCA-analysed clause and see if you can figure out what type of phrase each is.

1. (S My horrible brother)—noun phrase
2. (V has thrown)—verb phrase
3. (C my favourite blocks)—noun phrase or adjective phrase?
4. (A in the bin)—adverb or prepositional phrase?
5. (A again)—adverb or prepositional phrase?

Did you know the answers to 3, 4 and 5? Or did you have to guess? Here are the answers:

3. (C my favourite blocks)—noun phrase
4. (A in the bin)—prepositional phrase
5. (A again)—adverb phrase

Here are some intuitive ways of figuring out the type of phrase if you didn't know or couldn't guess.

Noun phrases (as we've learned) can be replaced by pronouns.

*He has thrown **them** in the bin again*

Prepositional phrases (almost) always take the form of preposition followed by noun phrase. (Don't forget: phrases can hang out inside other phrases, like Russian dolls.)

[in (preposition)] [the bin (noun phrase)]

And you know that *the bin* is a noun phrase because it can be replaced by the pronoun *it*. (*My horrible brother has thrown my favourite blocks in **it** again!*)

No, *you're* a preposition!

How do you know whether something's a preposition? I like to encourage students to get a feel for where prepositions show up, which is always in prepositional phrases. I give them a noun phrase (*the bin*) and then ask them to fill the slot before *the bin* with as many prepositions as they can think of. I get them going with examples like **under** *the bin,* **beside** *the bin,* and it's not long before they're producing prepositions left, right and centre. **By** *the bin,* **around** *the bin,* **near** *the bin,* **over** *the bin,* etc.

Prepositions are the word classes that are most likely to make people break out into a cold sweat, but I like them because they're so predictable. They show up in prepositional phrases, which (almost) always take the form preposition + noun phrase.[63]

Those crazy noun phrases

OK, so what about noun phrases? We've determined that they can be replaced with pronouns, but what's their structure?

Annoyingly for the grammar teacher, delightfully for the creative writer, they can take any number of forms. They can contain every other type of phrase. They can contain clauses. They can contain more than one clause.

They can be compound. Remember this clause that we had so much fun with earlier?

The snivelling excuse for a sibling that my parents produced without my approval will have embezzled those few humble tokens that I dare call my own without the smallest hint of remorse

The question-tag probe will point us to the subject without much trouble, and we know now that the subject is going to be a noun phrase. So let's have closer look at this noun phrase, shall we?

Noun phrase: *The snivelling excuse for a sibling that my parents produced without my approval*

When we "open the box" of this phrase we find an adjective phrase, a couple of prepositional phrases, a few more noun phrases, and a relative clause. Talk about advanced level!

I always make sure my students are aware of how complicated and embedded noun phrases can be. Then I get them to focus on a very simple structure that noun phrases can sometimes take.

Determiner—adjective phrase—noun.

And the adjective phrases I start with are always just one adjective.

For instance:

[My (determiner)] [horrible (adjective phrase)] [brother (noun)]
[My (determiner)] [favourite (adjective phrase)] [blocks (noun)]

Determiner shmeterminer

And then we explore determiners in the same way we played with prepositions. We look to all the other words that could go in the determiner slot. *Her horrible brother, a horrible brother, this horrible brother, that horrible brother, the horrible brother. His favourite blocks, those favourite blocks, these favourite blocks, their favourite blocks.*

And bingo! We've got a feel for what a determiner is.

But wait! I hear you say. *Are all of those words determiners? Aren't some of them* (her, his, their) *pronouns? And aren't some of them* (a, the) *articles?*

I tip my hat to your impressive metalinguistic knowledge. Determiner is an umbrella term that encompasses articles (*a, an, the*), demonstratives (such as *this, that, those, these*) and possessive pronouns (*my, her, his, its, your, our* and *their*). I prefer to teach the umbrella terms because they're easier to access intuitively. I figure, if ever I need to know a more precise term like *distal demonstrative*, I can always google it.

Nothing scary about adjectives and nouns

Usually my own students are pretty OK with adjectives and nouns, but if they find something that stumps them, I just get them to check it against the determiner—adjective phrase—noun pattern to see if it fits. Sometimes abstract nouns can trip people up (e.g. *frustration*), but when we check to see if it works in a noun phrase pattern, it becomes a little less, well, frustrating. (*My annoying frustration.*)

Happily labelling adverbs here

Adverbs are my least favourite types of word because they *seem* like they should be easy to spot. Just check for words that end in *-ly*, right? Unfortunately, annoyingly, frustratingly (sorry), this doesn't always work. Yes, most *-ly* words are adverbs, but there are annoying exceptions like *likely, leisurely* and *timely* (all adjectives). And there's also a whole host of adverbs that don't end in *-ly*, like *yesterday, here* and *too*. And *so*, while we're at it. Some of the time. *So* annoying.

Here's my method for helping students identify my frenemies, the adverbs. I start with adjuncts. Adjuncts as we know are (most of the time) either prepositional phrases or adverb phrases. Let's look at our example again.

(S My horrible brother) (V has thrown) (C my favourite blocks) (A in the bin) (A again)

We know that *again* is an adverb phrase because it's not a prepositional phrase. We know it's not a prepositional phrase because it doesn't follow the pattern *preposition + noun phrase*. (It's only one word. And it doesn't have a preposition. Or a noun phrase.)

Now let's replace *again* with another one-word adverb phrase, maybe one with an *-ly* ending to put us on steadier ground.

My horrible brother has thrown my favourite blocks in the bin joyfully.

At this point I'd ask students to keep joyfully, but add more words to the phrase. Here's the beautiful thing. Every word they add to an adverb phrase will be another adverb. So we can say he's thrown them in the bin *joyfully, so joyfully, ever so joyfully, ever so overwhelmingly joyfully*— and all these words will be adverbs.

One more happy word on adjective phrases

We've seen that (most of the time) a complement will be either an adjective phrase or a noun phrase. How do we know which one it is? If it can be replaced with a pronoun, it's a noun phrase. If it can be reduced to one adjective, it's probably an adjective phrase. Have a look at this little clause.

Brothers are really quite horrible

The question-tag probe gives us *Brothers* as the subject and *are* as the verb. The *who/what* probe gives us *really quite horrible* as the complement. Most complements are either an adjective or a noun phrase. So what type of phrase is *really quite horrible*? Adjective, or noun?

Well, *really quite horrible* can't be replaced by a pronoun, so it's probably not a noun phrase. But it can be reduced to one word in the phrase, *horrible* (*Brothers are horrible*). This tells us not only that it's probably an adjective phrase (it is, actually), but also that the adjective in it is *horrible*.

The other words in the adjective phrase that aren't the adjective? Those will most likely be adverbs. In this case, they are. *Really.*

Word class v. art class

Do these processes of working out phrases from SVCA, and working out word classes from phrases work to create a fun, easy-going atmosphere in your classroom?

I hope so. If not, feel free to abandon these strategies! If you have your own favourite way of teaching word class, I encourage you to stick with that. Or combine your method with this one to create a whole new way. What I love about teaching grammar is that it requires me to get creative and think outside traditional methods. I hope by now you feel empowered to do the same.

APPENDIX 2
PASSIVE VOICE (BROUGHT TO YOU BY ZOMBIES)

Have you ever checked the "grammar" settings in your word processing app? I remember the days when I used to get told when something I'd written was in the *passive voice (consider revising)*. I've just discovered that Microsoft Word still flags the passive voice, but without using grammatical terminology. Now it advises: "Clarity: saying who or what did the action would be clearer."

Is clarity always what we're after? Not necessarily. Let's return to the scene I've been referring to throughout this book, where Elli's blocks were stolen by her little brother, Jake. Now imagine that Jake's had an unprecedented burst in his language development and can tell his clueless aunt what happened during play time.

Elli's blocks were taken!

If Jake utters this statement with just the right amount of righteous solidarity with Elli's plight, his clueless aunt may focus on the tragedy (the stolen blocks) and miss a key piece of data (who stole them).

Jake would not only have mastered the nuances of clause construction, but also the dark art of using the passive voice for the purpose of deliberate obfuscation.

Obfuscation is not what we're going for in this book, and luckily for us, it's pretty easy to get clarity about whether a clause is in the active or passive voice. It's especially easy when you know how to find the subject and verb elements. The process can be divided into three steps.

1. Find the subject. (We'll use the question-tag probe for this, as usual.)
   Elli's blocks were taken, *weren't **they**?*
   S: Elli's blocks
2. Find the verb. (Enter once more the question-tag probe.)
   Elli's blocks **were taken**, *weren't they?*
   V: were taken
3. Check to see whether the subject of the clause is the one who's "doing" the lexical verb. If the answer is yes, the clause is in the active voice. If no, it's passive. In this case *Elli's blocks* are not the ones doing the *taking*, so it's in the passive voice.

It's worth keeping in mind that the passive voice doesn't *necessarily* produce obfuscation. Consider the following clause, which showed up when I was describing the block scenario, above:

Elli's blocks were stolen by her little brother, Jake

The subject is *Elli's blocks*, the verb is *were stolen*, and since Elli's blocks didn't do the stealing, we know it's in the passive voice. But in this case we also know who it was who did the stealing, *her little brother, Jake*. The English language does not require the one doing the lexical verb (what's known as the *actor*) to be the subject of the clause. In this case the actor is hanging out in the adjunct:

(S Elli's blocks) (V were stolen) (A by her little brother, Jake)

And, as we know, adjuncts (unlike subjects and verbs) are grammatically optional in clauses. We can leave them out. There might be very good reasons, in fact, for leaving them out. (Especially if you're Jake.)

You'll often see, in passive clauses, adjuncts that take the pattern *by X*. (If you read Appendix 1 you'll know that these are prepositional phrases.) The person or thing in the X slot is usually the actor. The actors of the passive clauses below are in **bold.**

1. (S My enthusiasm) (V has been sparked) (A by **this new understanding of passive voice**)
2. (S Elli's faith in human nature) (V might have been annihilated) (A by **her brother's thieving ways**)
3. (S None of the exercises in this book) (V were completed) (A by **me**)

If you want these clauses to be in the active voice, all you have to do is rewrite them to make the actor the subject.

1. (S **This new understanding of passive voice**) (V has sparked) (C my enthusiasm)
2. (S **Her brother's thieving ways**) (V might have annihilated) (C Elli's faith in human nature)
3. (S **I**) (V completed) (C none of the exercises in this book)

Extra points to you if you noticed that the subjects of the first set of (passive) clauses became complements in the second set of (active) clauses.

I'm a fan of this three-step method of checking to

see whether a clause is active or passive, but it turns out there's an even easier way. A participant on the Refreshing Grammar course shared a strategy invented by one of her secondary students.[64]

If you can add *by zombies* to the end of the clause, and it makes sense grammatically, then it's probably in the passive voice.

My enthusiasm has been sparked by zombies
Elli's faith in human nature might have been annihilated by zombies
None of the exercises in this book were completed by zombies

Damned if that doesn't work just as well.

ANSWERS TO THE EXERCISES

Chapter 2 Exercise: Happy bracketing

You were only asked to put brackets around the clause elements, not label them, but I've included the labels here for the keen beans. If the answers weren't what you expected, don't worry. As I said before, this exercise is actually the hardest one in the book! When you've learned the intuitive strategies for finding each component, it will all become much easier.

1. (S My three-year-old niece) (V can express) (C her views) (A without difficulty)
2. (S People on social media) (V have been shaming) (C me) (A about my use of apostrophes)
3. (S Most of my students) (V couldn't give) (C a fig) (A about voiceless labiodental fricatives)
4. (S This clause labelling exercise) (V is stressing) (C me) (A now)
5. (S I) (V will be imbibing) (C my favourite beverage) (A as a result)

Chapter 3 Exercise: Find the subject

1. Eudora Welty was a Pulitzer-Prize winning author
   Question tag: wasn't **she**?
   Replacement test: **She** was a Pulitzer-Prize winning author
   Subject: Eudora Welty
2. My sweets-loving friends really want to get chocolates for Samira
   Question tag: don't **they**?
   Replacement test: **They** really want to get chocolates for Samira
   Subject: My sweets-loving friends
3. Writing about anger can be a tricky business
   Question tag: can't **it**?
   Replacement test: **It** can be a tricky business
   Subject: Writing about anger
4. The question-tag probe is changing my approach to grammar
   Question tag: isn't **it**?
   Replacement test: **It** is changing my approach to grammar
   Subject: The question-tag probe
5. M. A. K. Halliday calls the question-tag probe a "mood tag"
   Question tag: doesn't **he**?
   Replacement test: **He** calls the question-tag probe a "mood tag"
   Subject: M. A. K. Halliday
6. I have mentioned his work several times in this chapter
   Question tag: haven't **I**?
   Replacement test: **I** have mentioned his work several times in this chapter

Subject: I

Chapter 4 Exercise: Stumped on the subject?

1. Not sleeping the night before your 9 a.m. seminar isn't a smart decision
   Question tag: is **it**?
   Replacement test: <u>It</u> isn't a smart decision
   Subject: Not sleeping the night before your 9 a.m. seminar
2. Often it's difficult to power through a lecture with no caffeine or happiness
   Question tag: isn't **it**?
   Replacement test: Often <u>it</u>'s difficult to power through a lecture with no caffeine or happiness
   Subject: it
3. This girl that I was talking to at the bus stop told me that my clothes didn't match
   Question tag: didn't **she**?
   Replacement test: <u>She</u> told me that my clothes didn't match
   Subject: This girl that I was talking to at the bus stop
4. Lots of Lucy's dolls have personalities
   Question tag: don't **they**?
   Replacement test: <u>They</u> have personalities
   Subject: Lots of Lucy's dolls
5. Sometimes destroying your emotional wellbeing for the sake of finishing your assignment is not well advised
   Question tag: is **it**?
   Replacement test: Sometimes <u>it</u> is not well

advised
Subject: destroying your emotional wellbeing for the sake of finishing your assignment

Chapter 5 Exercise: Give me a sentence, any sentence

1. Jay has been chanting about choosing cheese
   Question tag: hasn't he?
   Verb element: has been chanting
2. The other children will not join the cheese chant
   Question tag: will they?
   Verb element: will not join
3. Charlie the Chosen Champion of Chile is charging chivalrously into combat
   Question tag: isn't he?
   Verb element: is charging
4. The juicy chameleon was choking jubilantly on just one chargrilled chicken nugget
   Question tag: wasn't it?
   Verb element: was choking
5. The Cheesy Chimpanzees must have been jamming justifiably to Jazzman
   Question tag: mustn't they?
   Verb element: must have been jamming
6. Charlie and Jill are joyfully jumping
   Question tag: aren't they?
   Verb element: are jumping

Chapter 6 Exercise: Finite and dandy

1. Just a poet, standing in front of a question-tag probe, wondering what it can do for me

Question tag: aren't I?[65] or wasn't I?
That there are two possible question tags shows this to be a **non-finite clause.**
Finite versions: *I am* (or *I was*) *just a poet, standing in front of a question-tag probe, wondering what it can do for me*

2. Feeling pretty confident about subjects, still quite tense about verbs
   Question tag: aren't I/you/they? or isn't he/she? or wasn't I/he/she? or weren't you/they?
   That there are several possible question tags shows this to be a **non-finite clause.**
   Finite versions: *I am* (or *I was*) *feeling pretty confident about subjects, still quite tense about verbs; She/he is* (or *She/he was*) *feeling ...; You/they are* (or *you/they were*) *feeling...*

3. Getting back into the creative zone will not be easy for me
   Question tag: will it?
   That there's only one possible question tag shows this to be a **finite clause.** The subject is *Getting back into the creative zone* and the verb is *will not be.*
   Non-finite version? There are lots of ways you could make this non-finite. Here's one: *Me, not finding it easy to get back into the creative zone*

4. Surely screaming for ice cream isn't necessary
   Question tag: is it?
   That there's only one possible question tag shows this to be a **finite clause.** The subject is *screaming for ice cream* and the verb is *isn't.*
   Non-finite version? There are lots of ways

you could make this non-finite. Here's one: *Unnecessarily screaming for ice cream*

5. Disappointed about kids who refuse to follow simple instructions about staying out of her writing sanctuary
Question tag: isn't she? or wasn't she?
That there are two possible question tags shows this to be a **non-finite clause**.[66]
Finite versions: *She is* (or *she was*) *disappointed about kids who refuse to follow simple instructions about staying out of her writing sanctuary*

Chapter 7 Exercise: All tensed up and nowhere to go

1. George's dog has been saying *GRRR* quite a lot recently
   Question tag: hasn't he? (or she/it)
   Subject: George's dog
   Verb: has been saying
   Tense: present
   Clause rewritten in the past tense: *George's dog* **had** *been saying* GRRR *quite a lot recently*
2. Fido clearly had things to talk about
   Question tag: didn't he?
   Subject: Fido
   Verb: had
   Tense: past
   Clause rewritten in the present tense: *Fido clearly* **has** *things to talk about*
3. I have never heard the song "Strangers in the Night"
   Question tag: have I?

Subject: I
Verb: have heard
Tense: present
Clause rewritten in the past tense: I had never heard the song "Strangers in the Night"

4. That's making it difficult to remember the primary auxiliaries
   Question tag: isn't it?
   Subject: That
   Verb: 's making (is making)
   Tense: present
   Clause rewritten in the past tense: That was making it difficult to remember the primary auxiliaries

5. I wanted a catchy tune for the modals, too
   Question tag: didn't I?
   Subject: I
   Verb: wanted
   Tense: past
   Clause rewritten in the present tense: I want a catchy tune for the modals, too

Chapter 8 Exercise: "You're worth the whole damn bunch put together"

1. (S My father) (V gave) (C me) (C some advice)
2. (S I) (V 've been turning) (C it) (A over) (A in my mind) (A ever since)[67]
3. (S All the people in this world) (V haven't had) (C your advantages)
4. (S The white palaces of fashionable East Egg) (V glittered) (A along the water) (A across the courtesy bay)

5. (S The history of the summer) (V begins) (A on that evening)

Chapter 9 Exercise: Who you callin' junk?

1. (S All films) (V should contain) (C world-saving linguists,) (A in my opinion)
   Other places the adjunct could go: *In my opinion, all films should contain world-saving linguists; All films, in my opinion, should contain world-saving linguists; All films should, in my opinion, contain world-saving linguists; All films should contain, in my opinion, world-saving linguists*
2. (S A plumber) (V would be) (C a good choice) (A as the hero of an apocalyptic disaster plot)
   Other place the adjunct could go: *As the hero of an apocalyptic disaster plot, a plumber would be a good choice*
3. (S Alien languages) (A really) (V would be) (C fun to learn)
   Other places the adjunct could go: *Really, alien languages would be fun to learn; Alien languages would really be fun to learn; Alien languages would be fun to learn, really.*[68]
4. (S Grammatical analysis) (V... has) (A actually) (...V become) (C my favourite way to spend an afternoon)
   Other places the adjunct could go: *Actually, grammatical analysis has become my favourite way to spend an afternoon; Grammatical analysis, actually, has become my favourite way to spend an afternoon; Grammatical analysis has become,*

actually, my favourite way to spend an afternoon; Grammatical analysis has become my favourite way to spend an afternoon, actually
5. (S I) (V... would) (A never) (...V have believed) (C it) (A before)
   Other places the adjuncts could go: *Before I never would have believed it; Never would I have believed it before.* *Before I would have believed it, never.*[69] You could try *Never before would I have believed it,* but in this case *never before* would be a single adjunct.

NOTES

[1] M. A. K. Halliday and Christian M. I. M. Mathiessen, *Halliday's Introduction to Functional Grammar*, 4th ed. (London: Routledge, 2014).

[2] Thomas Bloor and Meriel Bloor, *The Functional Analysis of English: A Hallidayan Approach* (London: Arnold, 1995), 32.

[3] Would you like to hear more about my research on *like*? Check out Episode 86 of my Structured Visions podcast, "Feelings are, like, inside things," available here: structuredvisions.wordpress.com/2023/04/27/episode-86-feelings-are-like-inside-things

[4] You can find these at grammarfordreamers.com

[5] You can find these at structuredvisions.wordpress.com

[6] Halliday and Matthiessen, *Functional Grammar*, 140-2.

[7] Kim Ballard, *The Frameworks of English: Introducing Language Structures*, 3rd ed. (London: Routledge, 2013): 15.

[8] I've used a pseudonym for my niece and for everyone else whose conversations show up in this book.

[9] You might have spotted that *give back* and *take away* can also be analysed as phrasal verbs. Want to know more about phrasal verbs? Check out the FAQs on my Refreshing Grammar resources page: jodieclark.com/

refreshingresources

[10] Halliday and Matthiessen, *Functional Grammar*, 83.

[11] Halliday and Matthiessen, *Functional Grammar*, 65.

[12] You can sign up for my Grammar for Dreamers newsletter here: jodieclark.com/newsletter

[13] Eudora Welty, "A Piece of News," in *A Curtain of Green and Other Stories* (San Diego: Harcourt Brace Jovanovich, 1968), 24.

[14] Now might be a good time to point out that the subject of a clause isn't always the one who's doing the thing. The more accurate term for the participant who's doing the action is the *actor* (or *agent*). Passive clauses are good examples of instances where the subject isn't the actor, as in *She was being led by the hand*. *She* is the subject, but she's not the one doing the leading. Curious about passive voice? I explain it in more detail in Appendix 2 of this book.

[15] Ballard, *Frameworks*, 380.

[16] I explain the difference between active and passive clauses in Appendix 2 of this book.

[17] M. A. K. Halliday, *On Grammar* (London: Continuum, 2002), 298.

[18] If you'd like to learn more about these language acquisition experiments, have a look at the The Ling Space's fantastic video, "How to Test Language in Babies," at youtu.be/3-A9TnuSVa8

[19] Bloor and Bloor, *Functional Analysis of English*, 39-40.

[20] Halliday and Matthiessen, *Functional Grammar*, 140-2.

[21] Actually, there are 12, if you include *thou, ye, one, who* and *what*. The seven we talk about in *Refreshing Grammar*

are the ones most likely to be found in a question tag.

[22] Lewis Carroll, *Alice's Adventures in Wonderland* (London, 1866; Project Gutenberg, 2008), Chapter 1, www.gutenberg.org/ebooks/11.

[23] Would you like to join the Refreshing Grammar course? It's free and open to all. Sign up here: jodieclark.com/refreshingcourse

[24] Charles Dickens, *A Christmas Carol* (London, 1843; Project Gutenberg, 2004), Stave 1, www.gutenberg.org/ebooks/46

[25] By "always," I mean 99.99% of the time. Curious about the exceptions? Of course you are! Check out some FAQs on my Refreshing Grammar resources page: jodieclark.com/refreshingresources

[26] *Only one*—most of the time. Curious about the exceptions? Check out the FAQs on my Refreshing Grammar resources page: jodieclark.com/refreshingresources

[27] I'm including *copular* verbs under the category of *lexical* verbs for the sake of simplicity. Curious about that? Check out the FAQs on my Refreshing Grammar resources page: jodieclark.com/refreshingresources

[28] Halliday and Matthiessen, *Functional Grammar*, 140.

[29] Zadie Smith, White Teeth (London: Penguin, 2000), 4-18.

[30] Charles Dickens, *Bleak House* (London, 1853; Project Gutenberg, 1997), Chapter 1, www.gutenberg.org/ebooks/1023

[31] Some linguists would argue that *there* isn't the subject of these clauses and label it instead as an expletive.

I'm following Halliday, who labels existential *there* as a pronoun. His approach thus identifies *there* as the subject of "there is" and "there are" clauses. (See his *Introduction to Functional Grammar*, p. 148, fn. 14).

[32] It's more accurate to say that these are not complete sentences *in Standard English*. Some varieties of English, such as African-American Vernacular English (AAVE) have a feature known as "copula deletion," where the *be* verb can be omitted in finite clauses. The first line of Gwendolyn Brooks's poem, "We real cool," is an example of copula deletion in a finite clause, and it's perfectly grammatical. If Dickens had been writing in AAVE, "Fog on the Essex marshes" would also be perfectly grammatical. Unfortunately for him, he wrote this section of *Bleak House* in Standard English, so he might have to face the wrath of the angry red pen.

[33] In chapter 7 this definition will get a bit of an upgrade. We'll see that finite verbs are marked for either tense or mood.

[34] Charles Dickens, *Bleak House* (London, 1853; Project Gutenberg, 1997), Chapter 1, www.gutenberg.org/ebooks/1023

[35] You can read Roethke's "Child on Top of a Greenhouse" on the All Poetry website: allpoetry.com/Child-on-Top-of-a-Greenhouse

[36] The piece is called "Finite," and you can read it on my Grammar for Dreamers site: grammarfordreamers.com/2022/02/09/finite

[37] I have my own ideas about this obsession with seeing language as unique to humans, which you can listen to in Episode 56 of my Structured Visions podcast, "A story about language," available

here: structuredvisions.wordpress.com/2016/08/12/episode-56-a-story-about-language

[38] George Yule, *The Study of Language*, 4th ed. (Cambridge University Press, 2010), 12.

[39] Halliday and Matthiessen, *Functional Grammar*, 83.

[40] If your eagle eye spotted that I changed another verb in this sentence, you're absolutely right. I changed *stood* to *stands*. That's because another finite clause (*where the coffee bag stood*) snuck into the main clause here. This one is called a *relative clause*. If you used a question tag on it, you'd get *the coffee bag stood, didn't it?* and would know that the verb originally was in the past tense.

[41] Halliday and Matthiessen, *Functional Grammar*, 144.

[42] You may have spotted that this is a complex sentence with two finite clauses, a main clause and a subordinate clause. The question-tag probe will always point to the *main* clause in a complex sentence. To find the subject and finite verb of a subordinate clause, separate it from the sentence and treat it as if it were on its own. Then use the question-tag probe as normal. (*I won the lottery, didn't I?*)

[43] Maya Angelou, *I Know Why the Caged Bird Sings* (New York: Random House, 1969), 5.

[44] Sana Imtiaz Choudhry and Saiqa Imtiaz Asif, "'Ain't I a Woman': Exploring Femininities in Diaspora in Angelou's *I Know Why the Caged Bird Sings*," *Theory and Practice in Language Studies* 3, no. 3, 466–74.

[45] Angelou, *Caged Bird*, 4.

[46] Bloor and Bloor (*Functional Analysis of English*, pp. 37-64) call this an "SFPCA" analysis. Hallidayan grammar divides the verb (V) into F (finite) and P (predicator). I've avoided using the term "predicator" in this book not

just because it sounds like a sci-fi horror villain, but also because it's not a term most people are familiar with.

[47] OK, OK. *Whom.* I see you, grammar nerds.

[48] Or in some cases, adverb phrases or prepositional phrases. Curious about these? Check out the FAQs on my Refreshing Grammar resources page: jodieclark.com/refreshingresources

[49] F. Scott Fitzgerald, *The Great Gatsby* (New York, 1925; Project Gutenberg, 2021), Chapter 8, gutenberg.org/ebooks/64317

[50] If you too are an alien fan, have a listen to Episode 87 of my Structured Visions podcast, "What if you're an alien?" structuredvisions.wordpress.com/2023/05/25/episode-87-what-if-youre-an-alien. I've also published quite a few alien language stories on grammarfordreamers.com

[51] Ted Chiang, *Stories of Your Life and Others* (London: Picador, 2002), 111.

[52] Chiang, *Stories of Your Life*, 111.

[53] Chiang, *Stories of Your Life*, 171.

[54] Angelou, *Caged Bird*, 4.

[55] In this and some of the following clauses, *used to* is the finite element. *Used to* is one of those expressions that isn't captured by the question-tag probe. Here the question tag would be *didn't they?* Curious about *used to*? Check out the FAQs on my Refreshing Grammar resources page: jodieclark.com/refreshingresources

[56] Here Beth uses the compound lexical verb "came and dumped." Later she'll use a similar construct with "try and hurt." In these instances *come* and *try* are "light

verbs," and they're examples of verb elements with more than one lexical verb. Curious about light verbs? Check out the FAQs on my Refreshing Grammar resources page: jodieclark.com/refreshingresources

[57] Halliday and Matthiessen, *Functional Grammar*, 235.

[58] Jodie Clark, *Selves, Bodies and the Grammar of Social Worlds: Reimagining Social Change* (London: Palgrave, 2016), 63.

[59] Here I've analysed *backed away* as a phrasal verb. Curious about phrasal verbs? Have a look at the FAQs on my Refreshing Grammar resources page: jodieclark.com/refreshingresources

[60] I shared this research in a Symposium at Sheffield Hallam University on January 12, 2017, in honour of Professor Sara Mills's retirement. You can listen to my talk here structuredvisions.wordpress.com/2017/01/14/episode-58-communities-of-sara-mills/.

[61] I'm happy to share my first attempt at "doing all of it," a screenplay I wrote called *Grammar for Dreamers*. It's not very good, but that doesn't stop me from being proud of it. Also, it features a unicorn named Hank. Get your copy at jodieclark.com/screenplay

[62] You can prepare yourself for some of these exceptions by having a look at the FAQs on my Refreshing Grammar resources page: jodieclark.com/refreshingresources

[63] Curious about the exceptions? Check out the FAQs on my Refreshing Grammar resources page: jodieclark.com/refreshingresources

[64] Would you like to share yours or your students' nuggets of grammatical wisdom on the Refreshing Grammar course? Join here: jodieclark.com/refreshingcourse

[65] Wondering why it's *aren't* and not *amn't*? Have a look at Stan Carey's excellent blog post on the use of amn't in Ireland: https://stancarey.wordpress.com/2014/03/04/amnt-i-glad-we-use-amnt-in-ireland/

[66] You might have noticed (well done!) that there's a finite clause embedded in the main non-finite clause here, which is *who refuse to follow simple instructions about staying out of her writing sanctuary*.

[67] If you know about phrasal verbs, you may have (correctly) analysed this sentence as (S I) (V 've been turning over) (C it) (A in my mind) (A ever since). Want to know about phrasal verbs? Check out the FAQs on my Refreshing Grammar resources page: jodieclark.com/refreshingresources

[68] You might have tried *Alien languages would be really fun to learn*, but if you do that *really* stops being an adjunct and becomes part of the complement: (S Alien languages) (V would be) (C really fun to learn)

[69] Does this one work? *Before I would have believed it, never?* I can't decide. Thoughts on a postcard.

ABOUT THE AUTHOR

Jodie Clark

Jodie Clark is a linguist at Sheffield Hallam University and the author of two academic books with Palgrave Macmillan (Language, Sex and Social Structure and Selves, Bodies and the Grammar of Social Worlds).

Her fiction explores characters who discover (or fail to discover) how intimacy is embedded in the structure of language. The idea at the heart of all her work, both scholarly and creative, is that when people inhabit language, it transforms them.

Learn more about Jodie and her work at jodieclark.com.

Printed in Great Britain
by Amazon